NOT AFRAID

A Battle Against Leukemia

Be Strong & Not Afraid

Isaiah 41:10

Jessica Bibb Tisdale,
Edited by Maribelle
Sharpe Hoerster

Prologue:

Seeking the answer everyone seemed to be asking that day, I entered his bedroom just hours after his abrupt rush to the hospital. I looked around at his bed, unmade, his shoes piled in with his dirty athletic clothes now blocking his bathroom door. His pencil rolled off the half-written history notes as I backed into his desk chair. Surrounding me was the unjust reality that his once so peaceful, yet slightly grass-stained and sweat-soaked life was now buried underneath the enigmatic diagnosis of cancer.

On the dresser, where Jake had left his wallet and keys, I opened the third drawer from the top, mostly unfolded yet clean clothes, I see the shirt he said would be there. "Fat Boys" on the front and #44 on the back; the lineman's off field "uniform." He pleaded with me, rather than sitting with him in the cold hospital room, his brothers needed support. With his shirt hanging loosely on my body, almost like a night-gown, I found the camera, and caught the caravan to the game.

"Friday Night Lights" were not just a family favorite, but a town event. Everyone rallied, shut down shops, saved seats, repeated their speculations of the win and counted down the minutes to kick off.

Like a viewing of historical monuments on a carousel slide projector, each play of the football game embedded in me the harsher reality that was the unknown. The shout for victory in the crowd of purple, echoed the cry for mercy I heard in my mind. Number 44 was worn on the team's helmets. The audience wore button pins with his number. Signs held high with encouragement for the team who had to play without their #1 fullback and linebacker. Number 44 was everywhere, but where we wanted him to be.

Chapter One

August, two thousand and ten, ended ever so effortlessly. This particular weekend was nothing special. It was post "move-in weekend" at Wave's Z Islander; therefore, as a rookie leasing agent, I was ready for a break away from entitled college kids and their helicopter parents.

Home-bound I was.

With a four-hour drive ahead, and a surprisingly full gas tank, I left right after my shift, Friday afternoon. Finding a way to not sound like a home-sick teenager the night before, I worked up a detailed explanation informing my roommates why I wouldn't be around for the weekend shenanigans.

"My prep time at Blinn-dergarten (an Aggie phrase for the junior college associated with Texas A&M College Station) has come to an end, and classes at A&M start next week, so I figure I should spend time with my family since I don't know when I'll get to go home next."

Thus, a poor attempt at sounding mature and independent.

Afton, my good friend from high school, saw right through me, "Okay, Jess. Drive safely". That specific statement holds more value than initially thought by a third-party, our other rent check partner, Shelly, whose last name I don't think I ever really knew. Afton graduated with Jeb, two years before me. Their friendship always mirrored the siblingship Jeb and I were born into, and rather than feeling like the annoying tag-along little sister, I was appreciated as an individual, and out of it blossomed a raw, and incredible friendship. Yet, upon further reflection, it would seem to really anyone that Afton surely drew the short stick.

By far, I am sure she paid for every off campus- luncheon we were allotted in high school, she drove to any destination to which we both were required, and I am certain the car her parents sold to me in high school was worth more than I paid.

The second-degree burns from our lazy days by the pool left us standing for the better part of two days, the nights spent awake watching "Friends" well into the next morning while indulging in Thin-Mints which created a many-year disdain of that treat, and of course, the time we were sprayed by a skunk, was just some of the baggage I brought to our life-long friendship. I couldn't believe she was letting me live with her.

The drive to Mason felt involuntary. My PT Cruiser's steady hum over the nicely paved roads was almost like white noise. In preparation for normal questions asked by family members to recently dubbed "university student" I tried my best to think of some "pat -on-the back" moments they'd like to hear and unfortunately, I knew the four-hour drive ahead would not be long enough, yet I figured Mom and Dad should be proud of me whether I had it all together or not...

Yet, instead of highlighted "moments of Jess", the home- sickness took over the subtle white noise and my thoughts, and now, as if I had been gone overseas for 10 years, I pictured the faces of my family. As I zipped passed familiar land marks, I first saw Mom's face frozen in the position of "goodbye" when she dropped me off for my first year of college. Oh, aren't memories strange that way?

She always seemed to appear to have it all together but would be the first to tell you she doesn't. Somehow, she wears strength in her expression, but remains sympathetic, seldom shedding a tear, that I could recall. Something less likely expected from a lady just over 5 feet tall.

With the infamous dip coming up in the road, I slowed down, and clicked back to my own station, starring me. I tried convincing myself that I could tell Mom the truth. Working full time and going to school was kicking my butt and I didn't think I could do it. I needed help with some bills, but that would put them out, and EVERYONE knows, I'm not an only child… Just as fast as the thought entered my mind, it left. I knew I had a sibling that needed the money more than I did.

Besides, Mom has never complained about having to work several jobs since we moved to Mason. She also never failed to make us dinner in all the years we lived at home. She would listen to us while shuffling between each child's extra-curricular activities, dentist appointments, birthdays, or special recognitions… She really took care of our every need, attended every one of our ball games and cheered us on without an ounce of regret in her tone.

Trying to match my mother's same proud disposition, I took the exit for: Taylor… Just three more hours until I'd be rolling up in the dirt packed driveway to our home, welcomed by brothers, Mother, and my Dad's big bear hug…

I didn't realize how safe I felt in Dad's arms, until I hadn't felt them in over four months. Dad, Justin, much larger than Mom, with a voice that penetrated over all other noise, stands over six feet tall, and holds more pounds than he'd like to admit.

If it was thinking of Dad's voice or simultaneously headed towards hometown nostalgia, I replayed the many track meets when I'd be flying down that home-stretch for the 400-meter relay, focusing on breathing, pumping my arms, staying on my toes, and then finding my hole to beat my opponents to the hand off. The crowd's cheers would fill the gaps between the beat of my heart while my spikes ripped the track, and, always at the same moment, as if he was the only one in the stands, I'd hear his booming voice, "DIG! BABY! Dig!"

Then the crowd's cheers would fade back in, as I found Dad and Mom hopping up and down, cheering with all their might, probably just as breathless and high as I was from the thrill, and the increased rate of oxygen fueling the blood stream.

Somehow, they'd find their voices again when Hillary would blow past her opponents in the 800-meter run. Hillary and I often spoke of how much of a boost (much like in "Mario Cart"), Dad's voice would give us on that home-stretch just when we'd think all our energy would be exhausted from the meters already trekked behind us.

Hill, just 17 months younger than I, will always be the most intimidating and serious out of us sisters, yet, she was the best teammate and cheerleader to have in my corner. I couldn't wait to go to one of her Hardin-Simmons track meets, knowing how hard she was working to improve her time for the 800-meter run.

I knew Dad was so proud of her, but never made me feel inferior to my little sister's accomplishments. To others, Dad appears intimidating with his strong build, and even more firm stance for what he believes, but what some don't know is he is a big softy. Unlike Mom, I knew I'd see Dad tear up for one reason or another tonight. I couldn't wait for one of his stories at dinner time. Dad was great about leaving work at work, but notorious for sharing everything he read that day. He loves to read and remembers word-for-word what was read. Even if the audience isn't so amused as he is, he remains just as enthusiastic as when he started. I always appreciated that about him. Never caring what people thought about him, yet, he is intentional and honest and so very humble. Mom would often say, "he is who he is" and finally that made sense to me. I could see her smile, just like she had said it then and there.

Dad was adopted when he was a baby by a hard-working woman and her husband. His adoptive parents got divorced, and he pretty much had to raise himself. If it hadn't been for the kindness of his Dad's sister, Aunt Earlene, he wouldn't have known a motherly love like she showed him. During his high-school years, Dad's football coach took him under his wing. Dad always speaks so highly of him. He also talks about how his coach had a big family, and he knew, whomever he'd marry would also want that because he missed out on the entire family dynamic that I know I take for granted.

Gratefully, Mom felt just the same as Dad, and just within eight short months of meeting, they wed. (Advised by the afore mentioned to do as told, and not as done). Having seven mouths to feed within the first ten years of marriage could not have been easy. Raising seven children with very different personalities couldn't have been easy either. Some of us cared more about pleasing our parents rather than disappointing, but everyone of us knew how to fight and had no problem whatsoever pointing out each other's flaws.

Though some benefit came from having a house full of competitive kids; we'd always try to outdo the other, so in a way we kept each other honest… and partially broken-hearted. Well, except for Emilie, the eldest. She never felt the need to compete because she was already well above our maturity level. Although, she'd be the one to initiate fun entertainment for us to do with one another since that we didn't have cable and were too poor to go out.

We put on so many At-Home- plays for Mom and Dad.

I smiled at the silliness yet influencing productions still talked about today, twenty years later. She'd make us all feel special by devoting individual time for each one of us. I remember us all being upset when she started hanging out with friends more often than us.

We did not know then how to show how much we appreciated her. Now, I can pinpoint what it is about her that stands out. She had an ability to love over and over again, no matter how she was treated by me or others.

With one hour remaining in my journey home, I contemplated calling Em. I thought she'd be cooking dinner in her one-room apartment in Boerne after a long day of teaching her high school agriculture classes, but in the same beat, I knew my cell service would be unpredictable the rest of the way and didn't want to have to hear only bits and pieces of a conversation.

Thinking of communicating with siblings, I just remembered that Jeb wanted to know when I got home and to tell the family "hi."- Why is it that these simple instructions are so easy to forget?

I didn't have to miss Jeb since we lived in the same college town, worked at the same apartment complex as leasing agents, and went to the same church and Reformed University Fellowship meetings. He was good about giving me my space and letting me learn how to grow-up, and I was less-good about giving him his space because in my eyes he was all grown-up and I needed help, daily. Not much has changed in the area of me "looking up to him." When we were younger, he'd manipulate us younger siblings into finishing his chores, and to follow his made- up rules to the Monopoly and Life games which always resulted in his winning.

Though, I'm certain, volunteering to do his laundry and cover some of his shifts at work had nothing to do with the fact he got me a place to live, a job and an Aggie Mom, (a family from our church who "adopts" a college student), bought me a lap top and printer, and made me dinner twice a week. The game of Life must have taught him nothing if I continued to get all the free stuff.

Now entering Llano county, just 45 minutes from home, I realized that I didn't remember the last 60 miles of road... quickly I played back as much as I could fathom that might have been there or could have happened... to my recollection, I didn't hit anything or hear honking. So onward I drove.

I anticipated each landmark before it even came into view. I felt this highway, 29, in particular was one that I've traveled alone and with family/friends over 100 times. I remembered one time, the day we moved from Kyle to Mason in 2004, we stopped for a bathroom break, everyone took turns, then Dad let Charlie, our beloved family dog, run around for a little bit, do her business, then put her back on the trailer, hooked the chain, and we took off. Just a moment later, she wiggled out of her collar and either fell out or jumped out. Mom was following behind in Big Red, our family suburban. It felt like it took hours to dial Dad's cell number, for him to answer, and to tell him to stop immediately. Thankfully, Charlie was a little out of breath, but unharmed. Dad drove a little slower now and appointed the younger boys the job of keeping a lookout the rest of the way. I believe I was so traumatized for her, I asked to ride in the back of the trailer with her. Because that was vetoed, I rode in the back seat of the truck with my brothers keeping my eyes on Charlie. Being susceptible to motion sickness, I figured I'd muscle pass the nausea for the sake of safety for my dog.

I traveled memory lane even further back to the day Dad brought Charlie home in 2000.

We argued a little bit about what to name her, but Dad's word was final, and Charlotte was settled upon. Being German Shephard, part Chow and maybe another type of wild animal, Mom didn't trust Charlie completely. As a puppy, she tried to bite at Mom's face and showed a "rebellious tendency". (My ten- year-old self will not let me forget that statement).

Mom threatened that if she didn't shape up, we'd have to get rid of her. I thought that the safety of her children had to be the reason for such a threat, so I took it upon myself to train her. I spent hours on end with her every single day. She slept in my bed and kept all three of us girls up more hours of the night than we signed up for. Thankfully, my sisters were on Team Charlie, so they helped with little complaint. Eventually, she grew too large to share our tiny pink room with all three of us. She'd become very accustomed to the rules of the Bibb house. She never fussed unless someone was too slow to open the sliding door to let her out to relieve herself. The one acre back yard was her territory. She was always ready to greet us after we finished our school work. We'd see her face peek through the crack of the sliding door at noon, just like clock- work. All of us, besides Emilie, (her school-work took much longer than us younger kiddos), would play outside with Charlie, all the rest of the day. She wore many hats as six different imaginations and personalities tried to decide on the game for that moment to play all-together. She'd be a receiver the first part of the afternoon as we'd pretend to be at the Cowboy stadium with Emmitt Smith, or Justin Jr., as the quarterback. We'd converge football, to a game of chase, and she'd be the chaser, gently tackling us by standing on her back legs, and grabbing us with her front two paws. We'd often dig for treasure, and she was always helpful when it came to the tough, dry dirt. She learned quickly to share in our curiosity and excitement once we found something like an old medicine bottle or jar. Her tail would start wagging, and she'd run and jump in circles barking out "hurray". Well, we figured that's what she'd be saying if she could.

She learned which neighbors we welcomed over and would sound the alarm for strangers in the area. She loved to show off for our new friends. She'd sit, shake, roll over and play in and out between our spread legs. She'd do it for treats or free pettings.

Her ears would perk up and she'd squint her eyes when she heard "good girl." Even Mom and she had their own bonding time. Often, Mom would sit outside in the lawn chair and watch us play while soaking up some sun-rays. Charlie would sit on her left-hand side, nudge up under her arm, so Mother's hand rested on the top of her head. They were both happy like that for as long as we'd let her. But she'd come running just as soon as we needed Charlie to join in our adventures.

Dad was especially partial to Charlie. He'd greet her when he came home much like one of the kids. Charlie also knew the hour he'd come home, and that's the only time she'd quit playing with us. She had to be at the French door to see him walk in.

The nights it would storm, and the wind would howl, were the nights Charlie could spend inside. She'd sit through devotionals, movies or whatever it was we had going on that evening. Our favorite time was during Christmas, advent season, and the reading of <u>Jotham's Journey</u>. Charlie's ears would perk up along with ours, as Dad's used perfect story-telling voice to keep our attention. That living room on Dove-Hollow had so many stories pass through it. We certainly lived out every inch of that house. All nine of us shared a three bedroom-two bath house. The four boys shared a room on one end of the hall, and the kids' bathroom divided the girls room at the other end of the hall. We definitely learned to love one another within inches of each other. Not having a lot of money didn't slow us down from having a full-life. We never were in need of anything, and because there were so many of us, and no cable, we had no idea what we were missing.

If having many siblings wasn't enough of a distraction, having a cousin twin was a fun bonus. Mom has two sisters and one brother. Her sister, Natalie, had seven children also. Their ages ranged closely to ours. We always loved it when a cousin would come stay for the summer. Don't get me wrong, though we watched out for one another, and still try to stay involved in each other's lives, whether it's welcomed or not, our differences can come out in ugly ways. I was surprised we didn't have more broken bones. There were five boys and just two girls in the Hudson family. The days spent with them, the whole world seemed to stop, and we lived a child's dream. I don't remember ever stopping to take bathroom or water breaks. Fourteen children all at once was a bit of a challenge for an over-night stay, so at maximum, two cousins would come at a time or we'd trade one cousin for the other, then live a life as a Hudson or a Bibb for a week or two. They settled their roots in Mason and were eager for us to move back, and after eight years we did just that for more reasons than one.

Interrupting my days in Kyle as a young kid was the ringing of my trusty flip phone. It was Garrett, the youngest of the Bibb bunch calling from the house phone. I remembered he had just memorized my phone number as he wasn't allowed to have his own cell phone yet.

"Hey sissy, where are you?" Garrett asked, eagerly.

Not in Kyle anymore, I gathered my surroundings to answer quickly, "Hey buddy, I just drove through Llano. I'll be there in 30 minutes. Are y'all starving? You can start without me."

"It's okay. We'll wait." He sounded more patient that expected. "She just passed Llano," he informed the other listeners. I imagined Mom in the kitchen, Dad reading in his chair, and Jacob and Elliot finishing up the last of their X-Box game, "Madden '10," just in time to start setting the table.

"Dad said to drive safe" he added, still in his sweet, calm tone.

"I will. Can't wait to see you, Buddy." I wanted to speed up to 80 miles per hour, so 30 minutes would turn into 20 minutes.

"Me, too. Bye, Jess." Garrett hung up the phone before I could say bye.

Garrett was born in 1998. He was the bonus child, the unexpected surprise as some would say. He was the only one of us born in Kyle, Texas. He definitely was spoiled by his big sisters and brothers, except for Elliot. Elliot was two-years old when Garrett was born and was not convinced this new baby was any more precious than he was. Elliot's loose, sandy-blonde curls and curiosity got him a lot of attention both positive and negative. At only three years of age, he took apart the VCR, and then helped Dad put it back together. He wasn't just interested in seeing things, he wanted to see how they worked from the inside.

Both depended on diaper changes, feedings and play time and we girls seemed to be the first to volunteer. Jacob, born in 1993, two years older than Elliot, always seemed to be the child forgotten. You know, there is always that one child in a family that is less-demanding, quieter and is just as happy playing alone as he is with another. We'd call him Big Jake, partially because Dad is a huge John Wayne fan, but mostly because Jake was a big kid for his age. He was the only truly-blonde, light skinned out of us all. He tried participating in gymnastics with Hillary and me as we hoped it would help with his clumsiness and late blooming. But then it just became cruel and unusual punishment, so that ended quickly.

One day, we older siblings were determined to teach Jacob how to ride a bike. I think he was around six or seven years old. He had just received the appropriate sized-bike for his age and size. He grasped the concept of pedaling and breaking quickly but struggled severely with the turning part. He took instructions literally, so we older four, age average of 10.75, figured we'd give him step by step instructions. We established that he was ready to ride the bike the length of our driveway. All he had to do was ride straight down the driveway to the end of the street. Stop. Get off, turn the bike, then head straight back toward us, and we'd tell him which hands to use for slight direction changes. Eager to learn and accepting these terms, he took off down towards the entry of the cul-de-sac. The main instruction was to listen for "when to move the handle bars."

We all watched, admiring our own capability of being great instructors as he headed straight down the path before him. His momentum increased as he descended further down our sloped drive-way. Gravity pulled him slightly to the right, and within an instant he was now heading towards our neighbor's car which had been parked on the side of the street. A slight pull to the left of the handle-bars would get him back on the straight and narrow, but before we could call out this tip, Jacob's front tire and his upper body collided into the hood of the black Expedition.

After making sure all his bones were okay, we asked him the oh-so obvious question. "Why didn't you turn?" I will never forget the look he gave us when he replied, "I was waiting for y'all to tell me to. Why didn't y'all?"

He forgave us immediately and we decided to leave the bike-riding instruction to Dad.

Jacob participated in almost everything he could, track being the least favorite. One Mason invitational junior-high track meet he ran the 110-meter hurdles. He really was not good, at all. After tripping over each hurdle from the start, and then falling in between the hurdles, not once, not twice, but three times, Jacob finally had had enough, so he, instead of jumping, used the little karate knowledge acquired in one short semester, to kick the hurtles out of his way. He received the pity clap and a couple of "aws." He never competed in hurtles again. Instead he used his long arms and strength to throw discus and shot put. In reflecting on the past, the most change we saw in him was when Mrs. Dawn Hahn encouraged Jacob to perform in the one act play. This forced public appearance, though very entertaining, helped affirm and encourage confidence in him. That once shy, and awkward boy, now stood six-feet and three inches tall, weighing 230 pounds as a junior in high school. Mighty ready for some Puncher football by the looks of him.

Finally, I could hear the dirt and gravel crumble below my tires.

I nearly left the car running as I grabbed all my things and made it up the stairs leading to the back door. Family and friends entered the back door, and acquaintances only entered by front door. There everyone was, waiting for me in the back room adjacent to Jake's room…

My little brothers weren't so little anymore. I guess the bigger they get, the more they eat and the messier they become. With just the three of the seven children remaining at home, I could tell Mom lacked the girls' helpful hands, because it looked as though all seven of us were still sharing the same home. Be it messy, and smellier, I felt most at home and couldn't wait to hear how their last week of Summer was going.

Most of their voices had permanently changed, one was driving, two were still in Boy Scouts, but all three were sporting the purple and white of the Mason Puncher Football team, representing the varsity, junior varsity, and junior high teams. That meant "game night" was three times a week. In fact, that is all we talked about at the dinner table, over dessert and even into most of the night. Mom and I would catch up tomorrow, so I listened with as much interest as I possibly could muster after the first few hours.

Dad finally broke the long stretch of football talk and asked us if we wanted to do a devotional before bed. Twenty-three years of fatherhood, some habits just don't die. This "Bibb-lical" routine had me yearning for those simpler times, living in Kyle Texas, when Mom home-schooled us, and school let out at noon. When "playing outside" was a command rather than an option, or when three meals a day was a guarantee. As Dad opened the worn leather of his Bible, and fumbled through familiar pages, the three empty places Emilie, Justin (Jeb) and Hillary would be taking, made the whole room feel bigger. Though I had seen them just a month before, I couldn't help continuing to reminisce of when all seven of us shared the 3-bedroom 2-bath house with Mom and Dad.

Just like everyone else, we dressed in the decade, or close to it, depending on the garage sales and hand-me-downs. Now, the "little boys" have it so different, in small town America. Store-bought clothes, multiple pairs of tennis shoes… So privileged. Yet, instead of jealous, I was saddened because I didn't even know their shoe size. That's something I would have known, along with whose shirts were whose or whose foot-steps belonged to whom. The things that seemed so trivial then, now felt like pieces of me were missing.

My longing for the past was interrupted momentarily by Jacob, Elliot and Garrett racing towards the most comfortable seat. In the second it took for them to cross the imaginary line dividing the dining room and living room, Jake and Elliot joined forces against the weaker of the three and claimed their territory.

Garrett, being the youngest, never really can get a word in edgewise, but in the rare moments, does show a truly witty and charming guy, more mature than the baby-face exterior... I figured Jake and Elliot should be glad they're so much bigger. It's no secret, Garrett has dirt on them, well, all of us for that matter... and yet, rather than using it against us, he always shows how much he cares by doing just the opposite. So now, there Garrett is, with no cushion or back rest available, unless freed up by his bigger brothers.

Jake, rubbed the top of Garrett's head in a playful way while Elliot pointed and giggled his goofy laugh. Simultaneously during that exchange, I had remembered that Hillary told me she noticed in her last year at home, that Jacob and Garrett had grown closer, fought less out of the three. Elliot seemed to get along with both, yet at the same time, could get equally annoyed with both.

We had always noticed Jacob to be the more soft-hearted and patient of the three. Back when we were homeschooled, we used to see his tenderness as awkward and fearful, yet I think that had more to do with being the sibling sandwiched between the most dominant of the siblings. (Hillary and Elliot).

If I weren't kin to Elliot, I wouldn't know he was two years younger than Jacob. I noticed his voice was deeper and he seemed less hyper than the time I saw him at the end of last year's school term. Yet, he remained the goofy, clever and fun-loving boy I knew him to be. He had stepped into the role of quarterback and was working toward being an Eagle Scout. Dad praised his hard work and dedication, often. With no surprise, Elliot, was making quite the leader on the football field and apparently had no trouble building an alliance tonight with Jacob to defend the seating on the sofa.

Dad, of course, sat in the "throne", a much too large leather chair that took up a lot of the little living room.

We started with prayer and worked our way through the Apostle's creed. Dad, creature of habit, quizzed us quickly on the 66 books of the Bible. Jacob, Elliot and I realized Garrett didn't know them all that well. We muffled back giggles as he strained to remember the right book of the Bible following Lamentations. After the quiz, we recited a couple of Westminster catechisms, and then Dad read from the book of Daniel. We read the story of Shadrach, Meshach and Abednego. (We always appreciated Dad's simple approach to devotion. Never making it too difficult to understand but giving us just enough intrigue to question later.) Being familiar with this story, I only half listened as Dad brought us to realize these leading heroes' eagerness to serve their Lord, even if it resulted in death.

Typically, Dad would read from the passage, then would share the interpretation, then ask us for feedback. Mom would always listen quietly unless our direction was headed off track.

Feeling like we had it all understood, Dad asked us to put ourselves in their shoes. I kept reverting to the Veggie-Tale's depiction of this story and quickly tried to suppress my desire for chocolate.

"What's the take from this story?" Dad asked again.

Garrett was fighting boredom causing sleepiness. Elliot probably had a good answer, but was waiting for someone to confirm its validity. I felt my answer too simple; therefore, I remained quiet, trying to think of an answer that sounded more of a collegiate scholar than a high schooler.

Jake answered, softly, yet genuinely. Believing each word before saying it. "Well, we shouldn't fear death." He paused shortly, then continued, "they feared God, more than man, but trusted and loved Him more, too."

Dad agreed and added to Jake's answer saying that death should instead be a joyful thing. "Risking one's life for another, and to glorify God's name is commendable, and selfless. Death is just the first knock at our home eternity."

I looked at the faces of my little brothers. Garrett had been dozing in and out since his challenging quiz was over; Elliot studied the scripture, and then listened intently as Dad continued his mini-sermon. Jake noticed my wondering and concerned look. He knew how homesick I was, and that the last thing I wanted to think about was the death of others, so, he winked, knowing that this small gesture makes the biggest difference.

We spent the remainder of that weekend watching "Lord of the Rings", eating all the pizza rolls available in the fridge and sharing our excitement about future football games. Little did I know this would be the last night we'd spend together before the world we knew would turn upside-down.

Classes began at A&M one week after the little boy's school. I was relieved all my transfer paperwork was complete, but I was more stressed each day with the responsibility of buying books, paying bills, and making good enough grades while accepting that I now had loans to haunt me in the future. I worked every week day, plus weekends as a leasing agent, under Justin's supervision. He was assistant to the assistant manager and I was even lower in rank than that... who knew that could happen? I babysat when I wasn't leasing apartments, and the only extracurricular activity I was involved in was Church. With my peers, I masked my bitterness towards their seemingly spoon fed lives with quick humor and flaking out on friendship responsibilities. Giving just enough effort to keep up with my parents, and siblings, socializing was merely a means to an end.

Mom and Dad worked all week and attended every football game on Thursdays and Fridays. Emilie, 23 years old at the time, stayed busy with teaching 100 plus students at two different high schools in Boerne Texas, managing meetings with the FFA and planning classes and stock show bookings. Justin Jr. awaited the real world as he studied diligently in his last semester of his college career at Texas A&M. As a 22-year-old, he fended for himself. This meant working, paying bills on time and finding a good job, so he then could marry his girlfriend, Katherine. Hillary kept busy with track practice and was swiftly adjusting to her first semester in college. Jacob drove the younger boys, Elliot and Garrett, to school every morning, practice and back home for dinner. Jacob was positioned on offense and defense for the varsity team as the fullback, and linebacker. Elliot played quarterback and safety for the Junior Varsity team and Garrett played running back for the Junior High.

We were all caught. Not in an "oops" kind of way, but more as in a routine that had no outlets. We were going through the motions. Thinking very little past the challenges set before us, let alone the consequences of tried "normal" life.

CHAPTER 2

Shakespeare was extra confusing that day. It was only my third time to attend that class and I couldn't decipher between <u>Hamlet</u> and <u>Henry the IV</u> stories. I don't know why a professor would assign them together. Shakespeare in the morning doesn't seem healthy. I sat in the back because my professor used his cane to talk… I didn't trust his control over that sturdy piece of polished and stained cedar, so I sat safely from being called upon, and his enthusiastic waving and ranting over Shakespeare's "pure genius". Those are his words, not mine.

Next to me sat a cadet of the mostly self-righteous Aggie corps and next to him was his buddy. They were texting each other. I was happy to be judging their unabashed immaturity instead of Horatio's behavior in the presence of the Ghost. I checked my phone to see how much more time I had until my snack time. Yes, pathetically, I was trying to eat every four hours to get back in control over my weight. I wasn't obsessed or anything, but my "freshmen fifteen" came early and overstayed its welcome, inviting another ten of its fat-celled friends to stay. Besides, who doesn't enjoy planning their day around food? My food craving wavered when I saw that I had a text from Jeb stating that I should call him as soon as possible. I then noticed, too, that he had called me a minute before he sent the text. I replied immediately, thinking that a text would suffice for his overeagerness. I assured myself that he probably wanted me to work for him on Saturday and that this odd increase in communication was NOT AN EMERGENCY.

"I am in class, what's up?" I replied, hoping he wasn't going to tell me I had to come in to work early today.

"Leave class and come to my house." He replied not even two seconds later.

Knowing Jeb did not approve of skipping class, I immediately packed up my books and scooted my way out of class, feeling in my heart that this was not a week-end shift request. The cadet twins looked back at me, I imagine they were jealous of my unplanned escape.

By the time I reached the doors, I started running, nowhere in particular.

I've only heard of the sibling intuition. I guess I believed it could be true, but the knowledge of it didn't' go past recognizing who was walking down the stairs or knocking on the door… But on this cliché rainy day, I knew something bad happened to Big Jake.

"God, no. Please God." I repeated this over and over in my mind. My stomach dropped with the umbrella I was trying to open. Of course, it would be raining! I bent over to pick up Afton's umbrella she had lent me. I remembered then that Jacob had strep throat, but to my knowledge was still even attending school. Why would Jeb be so worried? I called him after realizing I had no car. "Can you come get me in lot 52? I rode with Afton." My words cracked with fear. What was going on? My mind was racing.

"I am leaving now." Jeb's voice was higher than normal. He'd been crying.

Waiting for Jeb to come around the corner, I felt cold. Attributing it not only to the temperature drop or the rain, but I couldn't seem to warm the fear in my veins. I didn't know that could happen. I have never really been afraid. Frightened, of course, mainly by scorpions and spiders. Nervous, oh yes. The minutes before a track meet or a basketball game made me nervous… but afraid… no.

Not until September ninth of 2010.

Chapter 3

I had forgotten it was raining until I sunk into Jeb's Jetta. My bags in one hand, and umbrella, still folded in the other. My stomach hurt, and my breathing was short, and still, I held my breath as Jeb spoke with tears in his eyes. He grabbed my trembling hand and tightened his grip with every word.

"Dad called me this morning. He told me to call you." Jeb gulped back more sorrow and pain and continued, "Dr. Eden, (our family doctor) ran a blood test last week on Jacob, and he just received it back early this morning. He believes Jacob has leukemia." Jeb's expression did not change. Looking deep into his face so stricken with fear and torment, my body then burned with anxiety. Jeb's complexion turned a faint red simultaneously followed by two small tears streaming down his cheeks. I clinched my jaws tight, placing my now free hand over Jeb's. I felt my throat swelling to the roof of my mouth.

Jeb broke the silence, "I am going to San Antonio. Jacob has been admitted to the children's hospital there." I think I was able to summon the words to tell Jeb I was going with him… Or he just knew.

We were going to a hospital, for children. I focused hard on grasping this concept. Jacob? Admitted? Where was the logic in this? Where was God? Why in the world would Leukemia be in our family? Is it genetic? What is Leukemia? I remembered every movie I had seen about cancer and what I remembered did not explain what I needed to know. Jacob was sixteen years old and made good choices. Why would he get cancer?

We had to go to my house to get my car. I had more gas at the time, (thankful to Afton always finding small ways to help me financially) and my tires were not as worn as the Volkswagens'. We threw together some articles of clothing and our campus minister prayed with us before we left. I didn't hear a word he said. With my head bowed, all I could feel was an empty space between me and Jacob. I closed my eyes, believing this was all wrong. "God, where are you?"

The drive seemed too slow. Time seemed to be getting away from me. What if this was the last one

Jacob lived and we weren't there by his side? My mind wouldn't stop fueling my every fear afore mentioned. I glanced over at Jeb, appearing a stranger in the driver seat of my PT Cruiser, although he looked a little more at ease now that we were closer to seeing Jacob. I so desired all our family to be together, as family should be in a time like this. Surprised by the hour, though time felt the most important thing, I realized this was the first time I checked the clock since checking my phone in class.

Only being 11:30AM, I knew it was Hillary's lunch break. The phone rang a couple of times before she answered, "Jessica?" (Hill never used my full name unless she was angry or sad) Hillary's voice was thick with worry and confusion. She sounded so scared. I tried to answer... My eyes didn't sting anymore. We sat in silence, answering each other's pain by sharing tears. In what seemed like hours, I was finally able to tell her to go home and be with the boys. "The boys" is a spoken title for Elliot and Garrett. Dad started it, and we all picked up on it. The first stream of tears subsided enough for me to finally speak to Jeb. "What's leukemia? I mean, I know its cancer. But, what is it?"

Jeb handed me his I Phone. He was always one step ahead of me in technology. "Google it, and read it out loud, but don't lose the directions to the Methodist Children's hospital."

While searching for answers, any answer, my cell phone rang. It was Emilie. I could tell by her ring tone, "I'm Bringing Sexy Back." Usually, this made me smile, but this time I felt relief. Emilie would know what to do. She'd have a plan for all of us, as always.

For the first time, I heard doubt in Emilie's words. Our words were few and straight to the point, unlike our usual conversations. "I am going to get a substitute for my last two classes. I think they'll understand. Mom asked that I go to the boy's games tonight. They are in Comfort. What are you and Jeb going to do?"

Awkwardly trying to make light of the situation, I was able to tell her we were going to surprise Jake at the hospital. Between my words, I felt inadequate. No gift could I bring, nor smile could I stretch, to make this better. I was not enough. We weren't enough.

We were helpless.

In the midst of her muffled sobs, I could hear her gratitude that Jeb and I were on our way to the hospital. I knew Em was taking this so hard because she was asking the same questions I couldn't bring myself to say out loud.

"Why, our sweet, Jacob?"

"Why cancer?"

"Are they sure?"

"How do they know?"

"Doctors can be wrong, can't they?"

Breaking her stream of unanswerable questions, I asked one that she may know, "do the boys know?"

"Not yet, Mom thought it would be best if they didn't have the distraction." Unknown to us all, Mom also had not told Jake at this time.

"Okay, Em. I love you. We will see you soon." Just not soon enough, I thought, after the call ended.

Minutes later Jeb's phone rang. It was Mom.

"Hey, Mom, it's Jess… obviously!" I felt silly for giving her that information as I knew she could tell my voice from Jeb's. Still, I was so relieved to hear her voice on the other end.

"Hi, Jessica. The boys have games tonight in Comfort. I need someone there for them as Dad and I will be here at the hospital. We'll let y'all know when we know more." Mom sounded very calm…

"Okay. We are on our way too." I tried to sound just as calm as my Mom, but I wasn't quite close enough.

"Are you okay, Jess?"

Mom asked ME if I was okay? Jacob is the one in the ER. Body invaded by stupid leukemia and she worries about me?

Feeling quite selfish, I answered any way. "Yea. I am okay. Are you okay, Momma?"

Mom avoided the question and told us to drive safe.

She had no idea we were on our way to San Antonio.

The rain continued at a constant downpour, no matter what county line we crossed. This seemed to trigger the "be safe" neurons in my brain to stay alert. Being led entirely by all of my feelings, I decided it was time to share with Jeb what I was believing to be true.

"I feel like… I'm angry…" A longer pause than planned took up the next few minutes, and finally I continued, "I am afraid my anger is… at God." Saying this out loud frightened me, as if God couldn't hear it in my original thoughts.

"That is expected. We get angry because we don't understand. But you have to put your trust in God and believe that He has it all under control." Jeb answered with such love and humility, but also, so quickly.

How did he convince himself of this? He was so ready to react, and reacted well, he did.

"Easier said than done, huh?" I asked rhetorically, but Jeb answered honestly and told me with time it would get easier, "go ahead and read that article about leukemia."

I tripped over the medical terminology and was only able to determine that there were two more common types among children, and both are very deadly.

We didn't say much more. He was deep in thought, and I was in thought about being in deep thought. I remember telling myself that I needed to pray and analyze the situation to understand and grasp it, but that was just it, I didn't want to grasp it. Once I did, it would make it all too real to me.

In my selfish, immature disregard, I sat. Quietly.

Hours went by and finally, we entered San Antonio.

We exited as instructed by Siri, focusing on street names between the sheets of ongoing rain with much difficulty, but it was distracting my mind with something else for a change.

"Turn on Floyd Curl and the parking garage should be on the right." I had the privilege of navigating. I spotted Garage 2 immediately, "there it is, to the left." Jeb turned left, before first needing to turn right. I saw the angle to the garage get wider and wider... "oh, I meant after we turned right." I said this quietly... I knew Jeb was like my Dad with directions... short fuse.

"Illegal turn coming right up." Jeb smiled as he said this.

I smiled to encourage him. We finally parked and had no idea what to do next. I would have been fine with asking the gentleman walking in between the portable buildings, but Jeb insisted on walking around the whole hospital until we found a tall, blue-eyed policeman standing by an entrance. We asked him where the emergency room was and instead of pointing and giving us a set of instructions, he escorted us.

What a friendly policeman... was it Jordan, Joseph? I really wished I had remembered his name. He led us to the red, curly haired receptionist who was talking to a mother and a young girl holding an infant. I felt sorry for them instantly. The young girl looked scared, and glanced back at Jeb and me, as if to say, "I'm sorry we are here."

I didn't know whether to smile or nod. I was glad they didn't take long to do what they needed to do because we were next in line. The lady behind the window wore colorful scrubs and fixed her makeup to coordinate with each color. In a raspy voice, unfamiliar to me, I told her that Jacob Bibb was our brother and that we really wanted to see him, but we didn't know what room he was in. I thought we were going to have to sign some papers, but she buzzed the door right open and said, "Room nine." Her smile was clearly on her face, but her eyes showed nothing but pity. I glanced back at her wondering what she knew that we didn't.

Jeb and I walked more slowly now. We saw room five on the left, room six on the right, then seven, eight and finally nine at the end of the hall. The glass door was shut with the faded, tan curtain hanging between the door and the room, also closed, keeping us from seeing who was behind the glass. We hesitated at first, then decided that since he was our brother, we had every right to slide the door open. At least, my enjoyment in breaking rules convinced me that we had every right to be on the other side of those doors.

I saw the doctor first, sitting on a rolling stool with a round black cushion that didn't look comfortable at all. To his left lay Jacob, with tubes and red flashing machines beeping in the background. Jacob smiled as I peeked through the curtain and waved. I walked in making room for Jeb to make his entrance; the room was small and stuffy. Jacob's face lit up even more while Dad introduced us to Dr. Geo, he had a pleasant face with a marathon-running shaped body and dark, friendly eyes.

Mom was sitting at the end of the bed which was clearly made for small children; her hands lay gently on Jacob's lower legs. I noticed just then that Jacob's legs were hanging off the edge from about the mid-calf range. The doctor was finished talking the same moment we walked in, so he left to give us some privacy. Mom and Dad looked just as surprised as Jacob did. Dad had tears in his eyes and told us that he did not expect us to come to the hospital.

Mom looked relieved we were there, but I saw in her eyes a look I had never seen before and hope never again to discern.

Jacob sat up in his bed as much as his comfort allowed him, "Thank you for coming, Guys. You didn't have to." I saw genuine gratitude in his light brown, almost tan colored eyes sunken and shadowed by dark blue, and black.

Jeb walked over to Jacob's side, "I wouldn't rather be anywhere else, Bud". I stayed put... I felt like I shouldn't move, and what I felt couldn't be explained so I said, "Well, you got me out of Shakespeare class! So, I should be thanking you!"

I regretted saying that as soon as it came out of my mouth. So not the time to joke, but to my encouragement I heard Mom let out a small laugh behind me. Dad had stepped out to make some phone calls.

Before I asked the question, I would have rather ignored, Jeb had blown up a latex glove like a balloon and began to stroke Jacob's face saying with each stroke, "you poor dear, you poor, poor dear" just like he had seen Jake do in a public performance of the Mason High school's one act play as Dr. Chumley in "Harvey." (Without said prop, of course)

Jacob laughed so hard the doctor came back
in to make sure everything was okay. He told us an
oh so obvious "medical fact" -that there is nothing like
comic relief to ease a situation such as this; and
quickly following with business, he added that Jacob
was due for a CAT scan within the hour. I decided
now was the time for me to ask the looming question,
"What did the doctor say before we came?" I really
didn't want to know. By that time, I knew it was
indeed, cancer.

Mom flashed a glance at the glass door which
Dad stood behind, and then her glance fell regretfully
onto Jake's body, as if transforming from rigid and full
to porcelain right in front of our eyes.

"On Tuesday Jacob went in to see Dr. Eden.
Until this morning, we thought Jake had a bad case of
strep-throat or mono. He has been playing football the
past couple of weeks, and though he vomited several
times during games, we never suspected anything
more than what can be expected with a swollen throat
and headaches. This last week, his symptoms
became worse and so Dr. Eden decided to take a
blood test to determine the sickness. That was on

Tuesday. The doctor called this morning and said Jake's white blood cell count was at 293,000 (the normal count for teenagers is 15,000) and that Jake should be admitted at Methodist Children's Hospital immediately."

She paused.

Our gazes no longer fixed on the eyes of our mother, but now, as if our own hearts were seeing into one-another's, only to feel exactly what she was feeling. Much like not knowing what your feet are doing when you are in a deep conversation with another; I no-longer knew what my eyes were seeing, but only what my heart was feeling.

Her words continued in the same manner as before... "Dr. Geo knows he has leukemia, but they don't know what kind yet. Apparently, there are two kinds, one being worse than the other."

I stood speechless, with disbelief swarming in my mind, though I knew it was all true. While trying to appear empathetic, and as if I understood, I was glad that Dad came back in. He could tell that we now knew, so he gave both Jeb and me another hug.

With little room left, he stood behind Mom placing his hand on her shoulder as I've seen him do many times. A small gesture, showing much about their relationship, never to abandon the other in times of need.

Mom broke this now awkward silence, with tears in her eyes, speaking to Jacob. Each word so intentional, I felt I was invading their privacy. "Son, I would give anything for me to be on this bed instead of you." Mom fought back her sobs but couldn't help the already escaped tears streaming down her face.

Jacob's eyes also filled with tears, just as fast as Mom's rolled down her face, "I know, Momma." He assured her.

Then and there it became real. We all wanted to take part of Jacob's burden. My eyes burned, so I allowed two small tears to cool them and wiped them away before anyone could notice. Dad's stood even more erect than before and focused his attention on Jacob, "Jacob, just when I thought we had to deal with this alone, prayer chains in our community already have knelt in prayer. We have to remember, though, that we will never be alone. Jesus has already suffered so you can give it all to him. God knows what you can handle, and he would not give you a battle you cannot conquer. Of which, reminds me of Jacob in the Bible, who wrestled with God himself. Big Jake, I know you are strong enough to fight this, because God is on your side."

I smiled at the leadership and hope my Dad had to share. Yet, it did not explain why it had to be Jake. To break the silence, Jeb offered more of that comic relief. It was easy to do with Jake. Since he was a baby, Jeb could always get him to laugh.

I worked up courage to sit closer to the end of the bed near Mom.

Dad, Jacob and Jeb were engaging in light conversation, while I was receiving a lesson on the signs of Leukemia. First glance at my little brother would show no signs of his body trying to kill him. Yet, as he lay there, Mom pointed out to me the hundreds of red spots, no bigger than the end of a ballpoint pen, covering Jake's legs, distinctively, right below the knees. "Petechia" she says, as if she had known all her life.

Realizing how much I didn't know, she explained it like this, "If there are too few platelets in the blood, basically means the body has trouble stopping the bleeding."

My uneducated mind thought to myself, "well, where is he bleeding?"

Meanwhile, she continued sharing each noticeable symptom more common the more she saw, like his swollen neck and pale skin, as if it was obviously cancer and not an advanced form of streptococcal pharyngitis. I kept hearing, "high white blood cell count" over and over again.

Each time it was said, I couldn't help but think it wasn't that big of a deal. Our white blood cells usually elevate to fight infection, right? Then why is it so bad that he has so many? Will his body not just fight it?

Feeling ashamed of these seemingly silly questions, I remained quiet. I continued to listen as she explained what she had been learning and finally heard the reason why too many white blood cells is a bad thing, "… so, if Dr. Eden had not sent the blood test when he did, Jacob would have had a stroke or suffered organ failure due to his white blood cells counting over 400,000."

I watched Mom closely, and as if she told me herself, she kept her mind from asking, "what if?"

Hoping I'd be able to grasp this reality with a little more knowledge, only increased my confusion. Listening to my Mother made my heart even heavier and more hopeless, I now was fully aware this was still anger seething between my bones.

CHAPTER 4

The doctor returned with less speculation in his voice and more of that annoying confidence that immediately proceeds what you may already know and definitely do not want to hear confirmed out loud, yet he caught more of my respectful attention with the inkling of hope I also heard, "Jacob, you have Acute Lymphoblastic Leukemia. Otherwise known as ALL. This is the kind we were hoping you had. You see, ALL is highly treatable with an 80% complete cure rate."

Amazed at how natural he handled news like this, I could feel my eyebrows furrowing... why isn't he more...no, I don't know, less cheery?"

"I am going to tell you what your life will be like for the next six to seven months. It will require a lot of hard work and discipline. Do you think you want to do this?"

A reply, so precious to our ears, filled the gloomy air, and opened our hearts to a new strength, "Yes sir, let's beat this!" Jacob smiled as he held his clinched fist in midair, his defined biceps and large forearms reminded me of just how big he was.

I wasn't so much shocked at the fact that my brother wanted to fight… I was shocked to see my brother smile, as if to encourage the doctors and family in the room. How could he smile after being told that there still is a 20% chance of death?

The doctor was sincere and confident as he went over the care plan that will more-than-likely offer the most positive results in the end. "For the first two weeks Jacob is to remain in the NICU. After those two weeks conclude he will have indefinite weekly checkups. He is to remain in complete isolation for the first two or three stages."

Apparently "stages" weren't a set time, and couldn't be predicted, because it all depends on his blood counts.

The doctor went on and even though there was so much information discussed, I still felt like it wasn't enough to solidify all this trouble. I subconsciously tuned the doctor out and thought more about Jacob having to stay in the hospital for two more weeks. We kind of just breezed past that bit of information, didn't we? It's the beginning of the school year. He can't possibly make up all that homework, and football practice... and this whole thing about "complete isolation?"

From what? From whom?

My day dreaming ended quickly when I heard the doctor recommend that Jake live in San Antonio. "If not, he'll need to return for Chemotherapy as much as twice a week."

He mentioned that there's a home-schooling program for kids with cancer offered through services like Ronald McDonald's House......

I searched the faces of my parents as they too listened intently, I am sure with their own concerns at the forefront of their minds. Neither of them could afford to stop working. How were they going to give Jake the twenty-four hours, seven days a week, care he needs for at least half a year and maybe longer? I knew for sure Mom would not allow anyone else to take her child in. But they could not just pack up and move to San Antonio either!

My mind was racing. I knew Mom would give up anything, her job, everything, but she couldn't. Dad couldn't. I could tell I was not the only one wondering how in the world this would be done. Normal would no longer be a goal to reach. They'd all have to change the way they lived. Jake couldn't go out into the public. Elliot and Garrett would need someone else to take them to school…

At just that moment, Uncle Treg called Dad. I followed Dad outside of the room. "Thank you, Treg. Thank you. I can't tell you how much that helps. No, I don't think so. I will tell him. Thank you so much." Dad hung up the phone.

"Uncle Treg?" I asked, knowingly. He is the only Treg we know in this world.

"Yes, he is going to the school to tell Elliot. I think it is better coming from a family member rather than by mouth at high school." Dad finished with a quick smile, almost too quick to notice. I believed Dad to be very much in control… He is strong too. As I was about to inquire about Garrett, a familiar face approached us from down the hall. Sharon Davidson, not only a radiologist tech in one of the branches of the hospital, but a family friend since before Emilie was born. I acknowledged her with a smile and at the same time Dad waved. Mom met her at the door and my attention was back on Dad.

"What about Garrett?" Concern couldn't have sounded more desperate coming from my mouth.

"Garrett? I'll have to tell him."

I knew this. I knew that Garrett would not handle it well. I remember he went home sick from school the first week Emilie left for college. My thoughts traced back to Uncle Treg. He is a good man too. He thought about all this, before we could. I wanted to hug Uncle Treg right there and then.

Jeb came out of the room and asked Dad if he wanted lunch. As if he had to ask... we both knew the answer and smiled when Dad said yes. Some normalcy still peeked through the grim future ahead.

"Well, Jacob is not allowed to eat, so let's try and keep the temptation from him. I overheard Sharon tell Mom that there is a Chick-Fil-A about two blocks from Floyd Curl. Jess and I will go and pick up some lunch." In the same tone, Jeb asked Dad if he wanted a combo.

"Perfect, son. Here, let me give you some money." Dad reached into his left, front pocket for his wallet. Jeb stopped him before Dad pulled it out. "Just got paid." Jeb hinted a slight smile, but in that small moment, more was said between them that I believe only a son and father would understand.

As we crossed several cross walks, and waited on traffic, not much was said between us, now alone again. I remember wondering if Jeb was thinking what I was thinking.

I couldn't help but realize that outside the hospital, life was normal. Life was fast... and the only time it stopped was for a red light. The feeling of disappointment slowly filled my feeling of emptiness. I was guilty of this too. I never cared before who was walking or driving next to me. Their stories couldn't possibly be as important as mine. I realized again how selfish I have been, not just now, but every single day of my life. Chick-Fil-A seemed way too far for walking distance as I noticed how hungry I had become... All the sudden, the quietness was annoying. I was not grateful for all the time I had to think.

I felt eyes on us as we ordered different kinds of chicken and walked back to the hospital. I could feel Jeb's discomfort, too. It took us all of 30 minutes to return and fill the lobby with an aroma of waffle fries and chicken. Time didn't seem significant, though. Dad met us momentarily in the lobby. Again, not much was said… I guess we were all pretty hungry. Dad abnormally took several bites for each waffle fry; therefore, as he swallowed I was prepared to hear what he had to say. He informed us of the agreed upon agenda between Mom and him.

"The boys have games in Comfort tonight, starting at five. We were wondering if you two would go and support them. Mom doesn't want...ehem..." he cleared his throat and continued, "well, will not leave Jacob's side. We can all stay at Emilie's tonight after the games per her standing invitation. Garrett doesn't know, and we want to keep it that way until one of us can talk to him."

"Comfort's about 45 minutes from here, right?" Jeb glanced at his wrist where once a watch abided, and in the same glance he checked his phone. I did the same to mine but didn't look. Jeb rose and suggested that we get going.

Dad confirmed the distance with a look towards the north-west. We said our goodbyes as Dad tucked away Mom's sandwich for later.

Jeb and I remembered how to get to the garage, but finding my car was a little more difficult. We still arrived to Garrett's game with about two quarters left. He did so well as the runningback and those once so bow-legged legs made some great yardage that seemed to keep those little junior high boys rallied for more.

Once again, it was great to focus on something else, and the warmth of the sun was a nice touch. We sat near our Oma and Opa and Aunt Natalie and Uncle Treg. They were all so perceptive and sympathetic but in the same way didn't ask too many questions which made the situation comfortable enough. Emilie and Hillary were there, puffy eyed from crying yet gleaming with hope. Hillary introduced us to one of her track mates, Aaron. She had a sweet sense about her, and I was thankful for her. Hillary is always stronger in the midst of friends.

We sat close together, and I was able to catch them up on the latest. I recalled what I could remember, but Jeb remembered most of the details.

"Jacob will be receiving what is called, Apheresis later on tonight. This device will extract Jacob's excess white blood cells and return his own red blood cells back into his body the doctor described it as mixing red paint with white paint in a long tube. It would appear a light, pink-colored substance." I added the bit I remembered about the normal white blood cell count being between 5000-10,000 which makes the ratio of red to white much greater, causing the crimson red. Before I could finish my sentence, I could see that everyone understood that this was not the case for Big Jake's.

Elliot's game was in a different location in the small town of Comfort. We all caravanned to the field and sat next to each other, again, facing west. I remember because the sun shot directly in our eyes till it finally set at seven.

Before the game started, I asked Uncle Treg how Elliot handled the news. Apparently, Elliot remained steady and wanted to be taken to see Jake right away. Uncle Treg asked him if he thought Jake would want him holding his hand in the hospital or playing the sport they both loved. Treg described Elliot as a young man, "composing himself as much as possible until he told me that he was then going to play for Jake." Uncle Treg added to those listening, that he had felt Elliot collapse slightly into his arms as they hugged goodbye. Uncle Treg flashed his eyes towards Elliot, keeping the memory close to his heart and smiled, "he then thanked me and headed back to class."

Uncle Treg had also talked to all the Junior High teachers to make sure everyone kept quiet for the sake of Garrett. Hillary then told me she saw Elliot right after Uncle Treg. Hillary went to the school to actually tell Elliot as well. She was grateful Treg had already told him because once they met in the hall, they didn't have to say anything.

"This time, though, Elliot kept me from collapsing to the floor." Hillary explained openly while glancing towards our 15- year old little brother.

My heart ached for Hillary, and Elliot. I asked Emilie who she had for support. A sweet student at the time, Kayley Wall, walked in her classroom just when she was on the phone with Mom. Kayley didn't have to ask Emilie anything; she just let Emilie cry on her shoulder.

As the boys lined up for the kick off, everyone noticed the same thing I did. On Elliot's helmet was the number 44. On the wrist of his teammates was the same number, the number of Jacob's football jersey.

Elliot looked like a quarterback should: poised, strong and like a leader. Unknown to us, Elliot made a special request from his teammates. He had felt confident that this game was in their control, and felt they could score over 30 points, but if they moved the ball more and timed it just right, they could probably hit 44, in honor of Jake.

Those boys started the second half like they started the first half.

As the game continued on, Garrett sat away from us all. He knew something was wrong and didn't appreciate that everyone was acting as though there wasn't. Jeb noticed first the displacement, and the pain then became clear on Garrett's face, it was a lot like all of ours had been initially. Emilie tried to comfort him by her warm hugs and loving tone, but Garrett needed to know more than that. Jeb decided to tell him everything, we had been whispering around him. He pulled Garrett from the crowd and explained to him the dreadful news of our brother. I heard Jeb over the cheering crowd, not because he was speaking loudly, but because with each word it became more and more real again.

Jeb placed his hand on Garrett's shoulder and knelt down to the level of his big, brown, worried eyes. "Garrett, do you know what the white blood cells do in your body?"

He nodded.

Jeb waited a moment, knowing that the silence would force Garrett to speak up. And sure enough, he did. "They fight infections." Garrett put this as a matter of fact and stared back into Jeb's eyes.

Surprised, Jeb continued. "Wow, I had no idea you were so smart." Jeb waited for Garrett to smile, and then he continued.

"If there are too many white blood cells, then that means something is very wrong. And that is what is going on with Jacob's body." Jeb swallowed back tears.

As Garrett listened intently, my mind drifted back to the football game. I spotted Elliot behind his linemen. I heard his voice, deep and steady, "Down! Set!" the third command drowned out by pads crashed together and Elliot looked for the open receiver… they were covered. I feared for Elliot's once broken collarbone, as a huge defensive end charged towards my little brother. In return, Elliot bolted toward the end zone and blew past defending boys larger than him. He rammed his way up the middle and outran everyone once he broke free.

Touchdown!

I stood up and yelled the praises towards my brother and his team. The town and the family were so impressed by Elliot's performance. How was he even playing considering the circumstances? I wondered this just as much as the spectators on the visitor's side… my attention drifted back to Jeb and Garrett.

"Leukemia is a blood cancer. God has already granted us grace, and Jacob is already doing much better. There is an 80 to 90 percent chance Jacob will be cancer- free after all his treatments." Jeb offered a little more excitement than what he felt.

"But that means there is more than a 10 percent chance that Jacob will still have cancer." Garret looked down feeling the weight of defeat on his twelve-year old shoulders.

"That is when trust comes in. Do you think you can trust God to take care of His son and our brother?" Jeb's grip on Garrett's shoulder clasped tighter.

How could Garrett say no?

Jeb and Garrett filtered in between our family. Garrett sat a little closer now to the family, but still seemed disconnected. I sat next to Garrett and shared with him the "lighter stuff" I could remember from the hospital. He giggled with me as I told him of Jeb petting Jacob with the latex glove and Jacob laughing like he always does.

"...Jake's humor had all of us laughing in his hospital room; there was this nurse prepping him for the CAT scan, and as she was explaining everything to him, he said "CAT scan? But I am more of a dog person.""

Garrett offered one more smile, and I couldn't help to see how similar he and Jacob shared that same feature.

I felt I should assure Garrett that Jacob has one of the best doctors treating him... at this Garrett shrugged his shoulders. I too, struggled with staying positive.

We watched the last twenty seconds tick away with the score of 44 to 19, Mason. A victory which rested easily in the hearts of the players and the Mason fans. Elliot told me after the game that he was so shocked at the strength he felt during the entire game. "That had never happened to me before."

My look of astonishment stunned my own pride. Why should I be so surprised my younger brother has stronger faith in our heavenly Father, than I do? I looked Elliot deep in his light brown eyes and saw him, not only as a fifteen-year old football star, but through new eyes, and I witnessed hope. I held him close and tight. I didn't want to let go of the strength I felt from him.

Now, the rest of the family surrounded Elliot on the football field. Opa asked me how I thought Jacob was doing, so I took this opportunity to lighten the mood with another one of Jacob's playful interactions at Methodist Children's. "So, Jeb and I had been there a little while. We had just learned of his prognosis when a nurse came in to ask Jacob some questions. She went through the normal routine by checking off answers on her clip board. She asked him if he had any allergies. Jacob paused for a minute and said, nope, just Leukemia. Jacob's smile sealed his light-hearted attitude and the nurse couldn't help but blush and tap him on the shoulder." Before I could finish my sentence, everyone was already laughing making it easy to join them.

Elliot and Garrett left with our grandparents, so they could attend school on Friday. The rest of us left for Emilie's house in Boerne. Opa gave us money for supper plus some more just because he wanted to. Opa's eyes were foggy and deep sorrow came over his expression.

There were so many moments where silence captured us. Where it seemed the only right thing to do was to just remain silent. No longer were we caught in our scheduled lives we worked hard to keep routine, we were now caught in a silence so overwhelming and thick, only a miracle could slice it open again.

CHAPTER 5

The hype of Thursday night football felt like a completely different night just a few hours later. Time passed slowly for us in Emilie's living room and even slower for Dad and Jacob. Dad insisted that Mom try to get some rest, so he'd stayed with Jacob in the NICU the first night.

Filling the sofa, and extra seats sat the four eldest of us siblings, and Jeb's lovely girlfriend (now wife), Katherine. Mom's eyes were especially glazed over with weariness. Dark circles surfaced right above Mom's naturally rosy cheeks. Her voice cracked with pain and emotional fatigue. Yet, Mom still stretched a smile for her children as we sat closer and closer to one another.

Many difficult decisions had to be made, though none of us were talking about them. All we could seem to do was sit, quietly. Some small talk was made when Mom asked us questions about how we were all doing... but I was not alone if feeling that our personal lives mattered little to us, at this time. Who cared if we didn't like our jobs, or certain classes?

I knew I had made a decision of my own, almost as if it was another part of me entirely doing the processing, urging and encouraging, while the rest of me could be angry.

I watched my Mom again, as she listened to my brother and sisters, witnessing more pain than a child wants to see in her own mother. I searched for every opportunity to fill Mom in on what I had decided. I tried involving myself in the moments around me, but I had to speak up soon.

A voice now was louder than the one in my head, Jeb had been trying to get my attention...

"I was just trying to see if you'd email your professors and let them know what's going on. I'm thinking we'd head back Tuesday." He said this almost as a question, I know to be polite, but I knew it was imperative that he get back to class and work. He'd be graduating so soon.

I couldn't help but feel how difficult it would be to go on with my day to day life knowing that my parents would be struggling every minute of every day with tending to Jacob's medical needs, bills, the boys, and well, life during this tragedy. It felt like this decision had been locked in my heart since the beginning and it was finally time to open the door.

Rather than answering Jeb, I faced my mother, "Mom, can I say something?" Our eyes met and everyone else's in the room seemed to disappear.

"Sure, sweetheart." Mom folded her hands and placed them in her lap, as a sign of her giving absolute attention to me.

"I feel that I am at a point in my life where I can be of more help to the family at this time. I hope that you will consider letting me withdraw from A&M to help out with Jacob's needs. I wouldn't have it any other way." I was pleased I could finish my sentences with such confidence.

Mom sat quiet for a long time. Time enough for the living room and the people to come back into focus. I felt everyone's eyes on me, then on Mom, then back on me. I continued, "I understand if you need to speak with Dad, but let him know, I have every intention to do this." I was then scared Mom and Dad would not let me do as I wished.

Whatever remaining tears Mother had left, barely filled to the swollen line of her bottom lid, "I couldn't have you give your life up like that."

"Mom, my life is not in College Station, it is with my family." I didn't mean to sound so rehearsed, so I finished with, "and I can start right back up when Jacob is all better."

To my advantage, Katherine, spoke and informed Mom and me that the quicker I withdraw, the more money I would get back. Jeb and Katherine nodded in unison as they both confirmed this bit of knowledge. Mom looked more at peace with this and said we would finish the conversation with Dad tomorrow. I smiled at Katherine to thank her.

I woke to the smell of coffee and breakfast tacos. Emilie's boyfriend at the time traveled from Lubbock, over eight hours away, and made this special delivery before anyone else was awake. (there are those in this story with few memories shared and remembered, but by design, will not make new memories).

With full stomachs and not as heavy eyes, we split up again. Jeb and Katherine drove to Mason as the rest of us went to the hospital. The boys stayed with the Hudson family and our Aunt drove them to school. I thought them to be very strong for not having even seen Jacob.

Many rules were thrown at us before we could see Jacob in the NICU. We had to wear protective gear, if you will, over our clothing. The nurses told us to sanitize our hands on the way in Jacob's tiny room, and on the way out. Only two people were allowed in the room with him at a time, but the worst part was waiting our turn to see him. Dad looked restless, but still in control. I summed up the courage to confront Dad about the conversation I had with Mom the night before. I asked that he follow me out to the hall as I had a question for him. I reiterated what I had told Mom almost verbatim. His reaction was much the same, extreme gratitude along with this almost regretful sting... Not for himself, or mother, but a regret they feared I'd feel later. Still, he reached down with his arms wide open. I walked right in between them and allowed Dad to swallow me in his bear hug.

"Thank you, Jessica. Mom and I decided we could not do this without you."

I appreciated that they had already discussed this and decided together.

The rest of the day felt anew and upbeat now… we kept that way for Jacob… but the truth is, Jacob is the one who put our spirits into upright moods. Being with him made it more bearable to think ahead from all the trouble. He looked so healthy, almost like he wasn't even sick. I kept thinking that he'd just get up from that bed, get dressed and go back home in time for the much-anticipated football game.

Dad asked how he was doing. Without specifying, Jake knew what he meant. "I'm okay, Dad. I know my team will do well without me. But I do just have one request." Jacob looked at each of us making sure we knew he meant what he was about to say.

"Will y'all show my team support tonight by attending the game?"

Without hesitating we both nodded, yes.

He then continued shortly thereafter, "I know the adversity they've had to face, and I think with your faces there, they would play without holding back, knowing I am okay."

"Understood, Son, we'll be there with you in our hearts. Would you like us to film it?"

Jacob smiled and nodded once.

Back in the waiting room, Dad explained to Mom their son's request. She, this time, insisted we all go, but she'd sit with him tonight.

"We can watch it tomorrow when y'all come back." Her smiles didn't come as easily as Jacob's.

CHAPTER 6

As we caravanned back to Mason to put on our purple and white, and carry Jacob's strength with us, I felt sickened by the fact that life had to go on. Almost as if nothing had happened, "Friday Night Lights" is still a priority… Work, school, social events, all were of demanding importance… I hated this. But I had no idea what was supposed to happen, or how this was supposed to look? Were people supposed to quit everything just to stare at Jacob's battle with leukemia?

Little did I know, our small town had worked all hours of the night, and up to minutes before kick-off with tasks, both big and small, to express its support and love.

As we found a parking spot near to the Puncher Dome, I was taken back by the number of cars filed in side-by-side. Recognizing folks in purple was easy, but everyone matched in a completely different way this time. The Beatys, who own a monogram shop, made hundreds of buttons with Jacob's football picture, to wear to every game. They handed them out at no charge with the instructions to those who wanted to pay to give the money to the Bibbs.

We heard that the cheerleaders worked until midnight the night before to make a new run through sign that said, WE LOVE OUR PUNCHER, BIBB # 44.

We made our way to the ticket booth, but rather than taking our money, Uncle Treg met us at the same time with already purchased tickets in his hands. His greeting even made me smile, as he told us that Aunt Natalie had to start keeping a log of all the meals families, teachers, ladies of the churches, and friends had been cooking or offered to cook since the moment they found out about Jacob.

Large, emptied pickle jars had been placed in every business to raise money for Jacob in not only the town of Mason, but surrounding towns as well.

A bank account opened as the Jacob Bibb Benefit Fund because hundreds of dollars had been passed from person to person to get to us. Tee shirts were being made, and the whole town pulled together and dedicated time and money to offer support, both seen and unseen. I couldn't believe what one small town could do in just one day. Our hearts expanded with the weight of love when the realization hit us.

Shuffling in our seats, shoulder to shoulder we all stood just as the team was about to burst through the newly painted run through sign.

Faintly at first, there was chanting coming from the Puncher football team behind the sign at which we were all staring. With each word, their voices grew louder and louder, and pretty soon the cheerleaders, band members and trainers joined in unison, shouting one word over and over again.

"JACOB, JACOB, JACOB!" Soon the crowd joined. Deep voices, high voices and small voices beamed through the stadium. My heart rose to see the faces of friends, family and strangers shining with so much love for my kid brother; the beauty of one town pulling together, to show love. It was powerful enough to slice through the feeling of loneliness and hopelessness.

The 2010 Mason football team burst through that sign with an energy that did not waiver until after the last whistle was blown.

I could tell you of every play performed by the team that night. I remember it like it was yesterday. People say that is the most heart they had ever seen from these young men. The radio announcer for over 40 years, Lee Graham, stated that this team wasn't just playing to win; they were fighting for a victory for their teammate Jacob Bibb. The scoreboard showed victory, but the players conduct, and performance showed much more than that… it showed love. A love so strong for their brother, they played better than ever.

The end of the game caught not only my family's attention, but that of the whole crowd, both Mason's and the visitors'. Both the Punchers and their opponent, the Comfort Bobcats, coaches, water boys, all huddled together and prayed for Jacob. Teenagers from different high schools came together, joining hands, lifting a fellow brother in prayer. Winning or losing had nothing to do with where those boys' hearts were.

Afterwards, the whole Mason Puncher team lined up and faced us in the stands and held up both hands forming the number forty-four. Mason tradition is that students, alumni, coaches and staff and all of the fans hold up a number one in response to the school song played by the band. Yet, this team broke that symbol for a new one, holding their fingers to make 44, high in the air, long and proud.

Tears of joy raced down the cheeks of people whom I did not even know, and those I knew well. Determined to capture each moment of love and support from our small community in the huge and small ways with the camera lens was my first and foremost duty... Jacob HAD to see this! At the Puncher Dome, it is customary that the families, and fans herd to the center of the field to offer pats on the back, hugs, and to take pictures, lots and lots of pictures... It is something so familiar and so normal to us to congratulate the boys on the field, and to be hugged by sweaty boys in pads.

After witnessing the great beauty of the way the town of Mason pulled together for one boy....my brother, how could there be a dry eye around? I so badly wanted to share in this response, but instead, I hid behind the video camera.

Opa surprised me by giving me the "record this," signal I've seen only in movies. He stood in front of the lens, awkwardly close, so I had to step back to actually see his entire head in my tunneled view. He choked back sobs and pointed his finger towards the camera, though, it was so intentional, it was almost like Opa was seeing Jacob in person. He told him how much he loved him. His lost, shaking voice was a sign of how hard he'll be rooting for him on this long journey...

I was moved by my grandpa's love for Jake.

Opa, or known in the professional world as Samuel Hoerster III, also taught dual credit history in our high school. I've witnessed him become emphatic with many of his students before. Always wanting what is best and going out of his way to keep his students on the "straight and narrow"- as he called it.

Hearing him speak in my camera lens, though more personal to me and my family, seemed an honest response to how he'd be for any one of his students. He cared for everyone like they were his own grandchildren. This being the case, he encouraged all his students to call him, "Opa", and so, they did.

As my focus returned to the world around me, I noticed a line forming respectfully out of view of the camera lens. Teammates, parents, and coaches had noticed what Opa was doing, and wanted to offer their support also. Hearing voices encouraging Jake along insured me that he would not do this alone. He not only had his large family, but every single person who had heard of his diagnosis, and his faith...

And still, why did I feel that this was not enough. Surrounded by hundreds and hundreds of people, I still felt empty, and I was not on the hospital bed.

Soon, the last of the cheers had been heard, and hugs given. The lights were cut from their source, and everything quiet and still again...

The darkness so quickly returned.

CHAPTER 7

Hillary, Aaron, Jeb and Katherine drove back to Boerne to stay with Emilie at her house, as the rest of us would catch them the next day to visit Jake. I was hesitant to return home. Looking back at the field where a victory, so incredibly fought, ignited a hope deep in the hearts of everyone for Jake's victory. It felt possible there, seeing the scoreboard made me want to hope this was all for a reason... Belief shone in the faces around me. Eyes met, so much felt, but so little said.

Dad, Elliot, Garrett and I filtered one by one back into the house. Our hearts heavy.

No one wanted to stay up and visit like we usually did post football game. We said our good nights with the plan to visit Jacob tomorrow morning, all together. There the boys went to their individual rooms right across from one another on one side of the living room, and Dad to his, on the other side of the living-room. The hallways in our home on Sabine Street seemed to stretch longer and longer as I passed through the dining room, kitchen, laundry room, into the addition in the back, or Jacob's room, the only vacant bedroom.

Reluctantly, I slowly pushed the door open, knowing fully well that he would not be in there. Upon entering, I'd hoped so badly he'd be sitting at his desk doing his homework and that this would all be a bad dream. Revisiting where last Jake had been before this brutal diagnosis crept along my spine as if entering a haunted house on Halloween...

Not at all feeling like I should be sleeping in Jake's bed while he lay on a too-small hospital bed with a 4-inch mattress and thinly threaded sheets, hooked up to machines, probably freezing and hungry, I instead sat on his chair in front of his desk. Next to his history notes, were his wallet, car keys and a receipt from Gigi's, his favorite place to get a hamburger, stamped a week prior...

This wasn't a nightmare.

Just one week before, Jacob's only challenges were a history exam, and paying off his lunch bill.

The indefinite diagnosis the doctor related hung true in every part of my mind. I begged out loud, to no one in particular, "Why couldn't this be a nightmare?" "Can't the doctor have gotten this wrong?"

_Deeper and deeper I dug inwardly for the right answer, yet the further I examined, no matter what I thought or what I saw, this feeling of overwhelming anger did not alleviate. Blankly staring in the midst of his lifeless room, I tried ignoring to whom I was angry. I knew better than to place blame, but who else was there to take it?

My eyes gravitated now to where Jake left his Bible. Bookmarked on his night stand… of course it was there. It would be the last thing he read when he fell asleep, and the first when he awoke. I choked back tears just thinking about how sweet and good my little brother was… too good to deserve this.

Eager to feel sadness, so I could cry, I just waited, anticipating relief that felt ages away, yet I couldn't shake the anger I felt deep within my being. No amount of logical reasoning, kindness from others, or memories alleviated the heaviness.

My eyes burned, but no tears rushed in to sooth them…

Through blurred lenses, I saw a simple life, based around God, school and football. But now what was it going to be? His world of endless opportunity and scholarship possibilities screeched to an unexpected and unpredictable stop. Yet, the rest of the world continued around him at an incredible speed. Everything he once considered his own was stripped away in one day.

How in the world could this be fair?

Why would God let this happen?

Shutting my eyes to try and forget the emptiness in Jake's room, I saw him again, lying on the hospital bed, with half his legs hanging off the end, looking up and grinning at me. Peace and strength emitting from his being.

Like a lightning strike, my anger quickly became disgust. This disgust was not directed at this deadly disease, nor the seemingly loss of value in life, but disgust with myself. I did not need a mirror to see how so inexplicably selfish I had become. Finally, tears streamed down my cheeks, solidifying my heartbreak and hopelessness.

How could someone about to enter into a brutal battle, that is, a fight for life, welcome it with a smile? How could I be so angry, when my little brother was so full of hope? Where was he getting this hope? An answer felt so close, almost tangible.

Listening in the quiet now, I heard not even the sound of crickets outside the walls surrounding, nor my father snoring. As if too weak to carry on with new tears, and sobs; I somehow was able to accept my brother's prognosis. Fighting reality was too exhausting. I couldn't will it away, nor could I change the day.

Yet, no smile stretched across my face when I thought back to Jacob's humble and sweet look of peace. Completely drained of all energy, I made my way to the bed now, picking up a few items on the floor to create a clear path. Amongst the random items was a 4X6 printed picture, of the best quality a 1990s film could make. Knowing neither where it had been, nor how it got there I recognized it was of Jake on his 8th or 9th birthday. The same grin, captured eight years before, steadied my hand. I studied the picture as if I wasn't present that day. He was so full of excitement in receiving his first bike, and as if the picture came to life, I heard laughter fill the room.

Sweet memories now flashed by, leading up to the end of the summer when I visited home right before classes started. I remember Jacob placed comfortably on the couch, saying these words, "We shouldn't fear death."

I knew back then Jacob was not afraid to die, and I knew now what his smile meant in the hospital the day before. Jacob is not afraid to die. The room no longer felt as empty.

Warmness came over my entire being as I heard a sweet reminder from a voice quieter than a whisper, but as clear as if it came from someone sitting right next to me, "He's still here". Feeling entirely too calm to not sleep, I laid my head on his pillow, looking at the wall opposite his desk.

There, centered amongst colorful and personal décor, hung a cross made with wood, and nails. The center of his room showed me where the center of his hope dwelt. Before I could help to recognize the expression in my heart, I closed my eyes, and smiled back.

CHAPTER 8

I always heard that in the quiet, God will reveal His will, but you just have to be quiet and listen... Fear, I know, kept me from listening. I didn't want to know God's will. I was afraid it didn't match with my own. Maybe we all struggle with sitting in the quiet, and listening, but I do wish I was a little more gracious during the transformation of doubtful curiosity, to trusting comfort.

Selfishness is an ugly gown to wear.

A change of heart encouraged me to see clearer that next morning. Today, like any day, God holds Jake in the palm of His hand. And as it is for all of us, Jake's life was never his own.

We left Mason for San Antonio shortly after a late breakfast (for the Bibb house), anxious to see Jake and Mom. Rolling into San Antonio, a road less traveled would soon become our direct path for who knew how long. Feeling the hour was close enough to lunch time, Dad stopped at Bill Miller's for some quick Bar-B-Q. Usually, this would excite the boys, yet Garrett complained of a stomach ache on the way. I, like Dad, figured it was nerves and that he just needed to eat something. As I tried to persuade him with the benefits of protein, he refused politely, and settled for only a cup of lemonade.

Meanwhile back at the hospital, Jake would undergo the second round of Chemotherapy, something still so foreign to us. As we were making our way to the waiting room, the nursing staff warned Jake that the medicine, not only causing nausea, is also prone to alter the overall mood of one's attitude.

Emilie, Mom, Hillary were sitting together in the colorful waiting room as we marched in. Settling in close to one another, Dad asked how he was doing.

Emilie giggled a little before she shared the little humor they witnessed this morning. "So, there Mom and I were, filling the extra seating in Jake's room, listening to the nurse explain the side-effects of the drugs. Having already been administered to him several times we were not surprised to find his reaction to feeling sick was a minor gripe or groan."

"He is the quiet and calm one," Mom added.

Emilie continued in agreement with the rest of us "when all the sudden, Jake started tossing and turning in his bed, tugging and pulling at the blood pressure cuff, voiced out loud with an inkling of irritation, "This is really starting to get annoying." but as soon as he said this, he looked up at Mom and me, and gasped, "Oh no, am I being moody?!"

The waiting room, filled with nothing but laughter for just a short while.

Each of us took a turn, with Dad escorting the way. Only two people at a time were permitted past those double metal doors. The day went by slowly, much like any time spent in a waiting room. We all made the same observation after seeing Jake. It was still so hard to associate him with a deadly disease. He looked just fine. His cheeks had a hint of pink in them, his smile stretched from ear to ear and he sat higher up in his bed than the day before. It was great seeing him upright rather than completely parallel to the white sheets. He not only looked deceivingly healthy but sounded so strong and happy.

The topic changed amongst us in the waiting room to the well fought game the night before. We shared with Mom all the support from the town, and all the work her sister was doing for us.

After witnessing Jacob vomiting all night, not having any sleep, Mother's face still lit up with thankfulness. "I could tell Jacob was eager to be on the field with his teammates."

Reality slapped my cheek, knocking me from feeling like a celebrity's kin, to a helpless helper. All the while we were consumed with the excitement from the game, Jacob was vomiting, uncomfortable and consistently nauseated with no relief.

Knowing Jake felt better today, I wanted to see him next and made that statement out loud. Or, at least I think I did... everyone seem distracted now with Garrett.

He had hesitated every time at the metal doors, changing his mind last minute, and returning to his seat in the waiting room. Since there were plenty of us to take turns, he got away with this a few more times.

Taking my time telling Jake of all the awesome support from the night before, "I can't wait to see your face when you watch the film. It is unreal, really!"

Jacob was always so good at matching other's excitement with his own.

With Dad hanging close by, Jacob gave my hand a quick squeeze and now focused his attention towards Dad, "I can't wait to watch, but I'd really like to see Garrett now, if that's okay?"

As we returned, Dad was able to convince Garrett to go with him this time, "He is asking for you, Buddy."

Garrett rose slowly from the seat next to Mom's. He looked sick to his stomach, but step by step was able to keep up with Dad's long strides.

Leading Garrett into the room, Dad stood outside the glass door to give them privacy. Garrett's eyes focused on the designs of the tiled floor. Jacob saw the face of his little brother, barely recognizable behind such fear and immediately reached out to him, "Garrett, come here, Little Man." A phrase used often by him when referring to his little brother.

In response to his big brother's call, still slowly, Garry stepped closer, just in arms reach to the side of the hospital bed. In the same motion, looked up at Jacob, finally releasing the tears he tried so hard to hold back. Jacob gripped Garrett's hand with what strength he did have. Not letting go, he looked deep into the eyes blurred with tears, fought back his own and whispered to him in a moment so powerfully their own, "Buddy, I don't want you to be afraid for me. Do you know why?"

Garrett tried drying tears, and let Jake finish…

"Because, I am not afraid. Alright? God is going to help me fight this and no matter what, He will be victorious!" Confirming these words with eye contact Jacob urged one more time, "You have to believe this, Little Man."

Returning the grasp, hand in hand, Garrett couldn't help but believe. In this instance, he also felt it his duty to not be afraid. Garrett knew, looking back in Jake's eyes, he recognized the same look he saw when Jake went out on defense and made a big game- changing hit. The same look he'd witness many times that had him cheering on the sidelines, proud to be his brother. He knew that look, the look of a warrior.

"I believe, Jacob."

They held each other in a strong- brotherly embrace.

Dad, smiled, having heard his young boys sound just like men, and quoted Joshua 1:9 in his mind… "Have I not commanded you? BE strong and courageous. Do NOT be frightened, and do NOT be dismayed, for the Lord your God is with you wherever you go."

Our Saturday spent in the hospital finally felt like time stopped for a short while. Shortly after the Powells (Afton's family minus Afton) entered bearing "What-a-Burger", a renewed sense of joy filled the room. Because of Afton and Jeb's friendship starting as Freshmen in high school, and now me living with Afton in college, our families seemed to have adopted one another.

Cindy and Mom seemed more like sisters, and Cindy seemed like another mom to me having fed me half of my high school years. Jeb, having known

Wade, who was younger than Dad, seeming more like a fun uncle, stood up to greet him.

They hugged, but before letting go completely, Jeb flicked the white collar that Methodist Pastors wear, in a friendly and playful way, "I see you dressed up for the occasion."

We all joined in with their laughter, knowing full well we weren't laughing at the bad "church joke" but more at the significant change it symbolized. You see, Wade just recently became an ordained pastor. When we first met him, he worked as a successful financial advisor and unknown to many, had a small career as a stand-up comedian. Of course, we didn't know him in his comedic days, but we definitely still knew the comedian.

He started pastoring the tiny Methodist church in an even smaller town just 9 miles from Mason, called Castell.

After our laugh, Wade asked to see Jacob as any good friend would do. Having volunteered with youth events, and attending his church, Jacob and

Wade had a friendship similar to that of Jeb and Wade, or Pastor Wade.

The visiting picked back up, while Mom and Cindy started passing out the hamburger and French fry feast.

Garrett was the first to dive in and devour a cheeseburger.

CHAPTER 9

As the last breath was drawn, no ambulance siren sounded, no screams or cries were heard. No more light shined through as the eyes shut permanently having seen the last there is to see on earth; mouth closed, as no more stories were left to be told, my great Aunt Hazel passed after having a very full life. Isn't that how we all picture dying?

Just one night following, the sounds of the NICU were disturbing and loud but were repetitive enough that Jake was able to use it as white noise and finally get some rest. Barely moving, with really nowhere to go, he lay there without complaining of boredom, fatigue or being homesick and fell right to sleep. He even slept through the nurses checking his blood pressure cuff, the sight around his veins receiving intravenous therapy, his temperature, fluids, and heart rate… Due to his drinking and eating significantly less than normal in the past three days, his visits to the restroom were few.

Dad was able to dose off as well, shutting his eyelids with his son's new position at the forefront of his mind, thinking to himself, "My tallest and strongest son, just days ago fought upright as linebacker on the field for a win; now lies on his back fighting for his life."

A routine fire drill at a hospital is a normal procedure, but hardly a "normal" something done at home and even at school. Both were jolted awake by a screeching alarm and bright flashing lights blinking in unison with the alarm. Now, getting enough sleep has always been important to Dad, but a 4AM wakeup call was not that unusual for him. Jake, of course, had no military training, so meeting the morning at such an hour for the first time under such circumstances was an annoyance. He preferred sleeping through the nausea rather than its aggressive nudges during the day.

Dad figured since they were awake, and safely assumed the rest of the hospital was awake as well, that it was never really too early for breakfast. Having made mention of this shortly after completing his thought, Jake quickly shared in the hearty desire for food.

Just thirty minutes to the west, using the few cars traveling highway 10 as our white noise, Emilie's guests arose to the aroma of coffee and eggs and bacon around 7:30 AM. Emilie, given any circumstance, was always the gracious hostess. Just as sleep wore off, and we began to wonder out loud how our brother was doing, Mom's cell phone started ringing as if triggered by our discussion. She ran back down the hall to the bedroom where she'd left it charging. Her footsteps stopped, and immediately after, we heard her voice answer, "Hi honey!"

We siblings in the dining room stopped chewing and talking and listened to the one-sided conversation down the hall.

"He did eat breakfast?" Her tone sounded higher pitched. "Uh, oh... oh dear, poor guy." Her tone dropped to just above a whisper. "Oh my, poor Jacob…" now knowing her empathy took over her tone all together.

"No more granola bars then?"

"Could he keep anything else down?"

Now she just answered with "mmhmms and more Oh no's." Thus, we all at the breakfast table searched each other's faces, more quietly than before, thinking the same obvious conclusion.

Her voice perked up, and grew louder, as she walked back towards us down the hall.

Dad's voice, sounding like one on a radio, filled the room. Mom put him on speaker phone, he hadn't stopped talking… "Good news followed his 6:00 AM lab work. White blood cells were down to 77,000! You know, just twenty- four hours prior it was over 169,000! His spinal tap also revealed no cancer cells in his spinal fluid!"

Cheers now overcame the empty spaces in the room, loud enough that Jake could hear on the other end as well.

Dad concluded, "I am grateful we are already seeing such positive results! Jake will be home before we know it."

Faintly, we heard Jake's voice in the background. Then Dad's filled the room again.

"… yep, okay son. Jake says hi! A few of his buddies texted asking if they could come today."

Now directing his voice at Jake, it sounded maybe just a click quieter to his other listeners, "I think so, if you're feeling up to it. How many? I thought just a handful had their driver's license. Ha Ha ha…" his voice just a click louder now, "We'll see y'all later today! Love all y'all."

We all said it back, one after another and heard both of them now laughing together.

Sunday afternoon came quickly. Mom had to organize attending her great Aunt's funeral and arranging for someone to stay with Jake in the hospital, so Dad could attend it as well. Within a few minutes of asking, Mom's co-worker at the time, Cristy, volunteered her time. Mom, and Hillary left for the hospital, so Hillary could say goodbye to Jake before heading back to college. She had assignments due the next morning and track practice to attend.

Jeb and I weren't due to leave until Tuesday, so we packed up and headed to Mason to also attend the funeral that afternoon. We'd all see one-another at the funeral, except for Jake. I could only remember a few memories of Hazel, myself, but enjoyed hearing of her past from her closer relations. The funeral was short and sweet, and naturally, we all gravitated together to discuss who was also on our minds.

Hillary first explained how hard it was to say goodbye to Jacob today at the hospital, "It felt like I was leaving a big part of my heart behind, and I wanted Jacob to keep it."

They have had a great understanding of closeness since Hillary's senior year in High School. Jacob could tell when she was having a bad day, and would always get her Root Beer and Skittles, her two comfort foods to make it better. But this time, in the most difficult time for Jacob, she could offer no comfort.

Dad encouraged her by telling us all how excited he was to see his football buddies. Just before Dad was getting ready to leave his room, two of his "Fat Boy" brothers walked in shoulder to shoulder barely fitting through the sliding door. You really couldn't tell Jake had just vomited four times that morning and lost five pounds.

Our farewells filled with more emotion than usual as we sent off the two Hardin Simmons track stars back into their care-free college life. Hillary said she'd be back as soon as she could and would call every day.

And every day, she did.

Two hours from Jacob felt like two days. Urging Mom and Dad to get some rest, finally in their own beds, did little to no good. Their hearts were with their son, and neither of them slept through the night.

Time still felt slow the next morning. Though we ate breakfast a little faster, packed the car in a bit of hurry, and organized car pools, schedules and the like, getting to Jacob was not happening fast enough.

We rushed only to wait.

And wait.

As we waited for Monday afternoon's lab results Jeb set up the video camera to the old TV provided by the hospital on one of those trays with wheels. Finally, Jake would get to see the Mason vs Comfort game. The rest of us decided to give them some space as they could forget about the results and focus on something more exciting. Yet, back in the waiting room we started using "doctor lingo."

It was much easier using WBC rather than saying "white blood cell" every time we discussed his blood counts, which was becoming something of a regular conversation, almost like when we mention the looming weight goal that we've all set for ourselves at one time or another.

In just a few seconds, our hours of waiting and wonder were over when the doctor told his WBCs were over 40,000 less than Sunday morning! Encouragement and hope filled our hearts immediately. Treatment was working!

But when would he be Leukemia free?

Shortly after the news, Jeb re-entered the waiting room, we'd unashamedly took over one half of the space.

"How'd it go?" Dad asked, after Jeb found a seat.

"He never gave any notice that he was feeling sorry for himself and the fact that he couldn't play. Instead, throughout the film, Jake would shout out cheers and hoorays for his teammates as if it was on live TV..." Jeb's smile looked sad, "and it was not until the end of the film did Jake tear up as the team lined up for the school song and held up their hands with four fingers to make "44.-made me emotional again..."

We all agreed as the re-capture filled our eyes with tears again.

"He didn't want to be emotional, but there were definitely a couple of tears and a bit of a tremble in his lower lip as he watched the team, coaches, cheerleaders, water-girls and fans gesturing in his honor. The real downpour came in the personal interviews at the end of the film."

I uttered with broken sobs, "it was my hope that he wouldn't feel forgotten or left out, but his teammates went above and beyond and showed brotherly love! It seemed a connection amongst teammates that I had only seen in "Remember the Titans"."

The common message poured from the hearts of his teammates. They told him to fight hard and get better soon, as his jersey is waiting for him. To be able to re-watch the support and love humbled our very beings. The feeling of defeat was conquered there and then. Jake was not alone. He could fight, and he would.

CHAPTER 10

Once we returned to College Station, Jeb sought help from his close friends and started working on plans for a campaign called, Play for Jake. The efforts were dedicated to raise money to help pay for bills, food and for many different medications. To our surprise, several activity teams across the state had already begun planning fundraisers in Jake's honor. Upon hearing this, I was convinced word of mouth is the fastest form of communication.

I started packing as soon as I returned to my house on Sarah Street. I told my roommates what I was going to do for the next seven to eight months of my life. They seemed understanding for the most part but told me I should think about it for a couple of days. Their hesitant support left me feeling empty and hurt, at first, but when I had some time alone, I realized they were voicing my own concerns that I was afraid to face.

I knew it was difficult getting back into school after quitting, yet I didn't want to wrap my head around the fact that I would not be graduating with the people I considered friends. I knew I was leaving behind an amazing community and a great church. I told myself it would be extremely easy to feel sorry for myself. No one would blame me if I had second thoughts. But, before I could begin to show any form of regret, I remembered the football game on Friday night. I saw my Dad's face, choking back tears. I heard every single voice of love and hope from the people of my hometown. I saw my Mom's hand placed so gently on Jake's shoulder telling him she wished it was her on the bed instead of him. My heartbeat slowed, and I felt overwhelming peace. I knew I was doing the right thing.

Though it was probably too late in the night, I called my "Aggie Mom" and asked her to go with me to withdraw from Texas A&M. She raised no question and said she'd pick me up at 8 AM.

Before I shut my eyes on that very long day, I called Mom to hear the latest on Jake's progress. Hope overpowered Mom's exhaustion as she explained the latest test results.

"Jacob's WBC was down to 5,700. This is considered the "normal" range. With the chemo treatments progressing as they are, his counts should be down to zero in no time."

I could tell Mom wasn't telling me everything, so I pressed on more "and" so she continued, "this also means Jacob will have absolutely no immune system. Risk of infection is high."

A scary thought to sleep on.

Wednesday morning marked the seventh day of Jake's diagnosis. His morning lab revealed a WBS of 2,800. His platelet count was 58. Unfortunately, this wasn't entirely all good news. Though his WBC was decreasing on schedule, the Doctors needed his platelet count to be somewhere between 140 and 400. A possible blood transfusion was anticipated to get Jacob's platelets where they needed to be. A common thing in the ICU, but something I thought would never happen to a member of my family.

I felt so far away and almost detached from Jacob. Though I was working on withdrawing from school for him, I felt like it wasn't real. I called to check on him, in between visits with my advisor. Dad told me that Jacob was put on a strict diet because they needed to be able to control everything in order for things to happen on time. I was confused about why, so I just asked what his diet was like.

"Thick skinned fruits were okay, but, fresh fruits and vegetables were not okay because there are contaminates found on them that can be very harmful to someone with little immune system."

Dad's voice changed from informative, to sorrowful. It hurt him to see Jacob's cheeks sink in from rapid weight loss. Dad's Big Jake wasn't so big anymore.

I felt stressed making life-altering changes on my own. I know Mom would have been more than happy to help, but I knew exactly how stressed out she could get, and already was, so I couldn't add to it. Leah, my Aggie mom, drove me all over campus as our friend Sara, navigated to the right buildings. First, I asked my questions at the Admissions office, and they directed me to the Financial Aid/Government Loans building, I told them the exact same thing I told Jennifer at the Admissions office, and they then told me to visit my advisor's office. Simple enough, right? If I had my own advisor. General Studies majors didn't receive that luxury, but Sara, a person to know because she knows every person, had a friend who was an advisor in the General Studies program. I felt as though doors continued opening up for me. With this encouragement, I knew I was doing the right thing.

Half way through the morning though, I began to regret taking out loans and actually accepting my enrollment at Texas A&M. I decided to take my deferment one semester at a time. My advisor officially dropped my classes for that semester and I was to call her before spring semester started. It was as simple as that… in the end. Before the final conversation with my advisor, my head felt like it was in overdrive. I couldn't help thinking of all the paperwork and stuff I had done months before to transfer. I remember briefly thinking to myself how much money it was all going to require in the end, but now, it will be like I never existed.

While I was dealing with financial issues way above my head, Mom had to arrange legal issues with the High School. The hospital offered a home-schooling program, but Jacob would have to live in San Antonio to qualify. The other option was to have his school teachers spend four hours a week with him in person to keep him caught up with the rest of the class. As Mom was telling me this over the phone, I was so glad I was not the parent in this situation.

Some of my peers tried talking me out of withdrawing; Afton and Sara supported me entirely by helping me pack, praying for me and wishing me and my family well. I was able to pack my belongings and get everything squared away in two short days. My employers understood why I was leaving and told me I could have my job back at any time.

At the end of each day I was away from Jacob, my thoughts went to how lonely he might be feeling but my beautifully large family did not allow that to happen.

Every day and night he had a new visitor. This filled me with such joy, I turned on my light and started writing in my pink journal Jeb had gifted me just a month prior for my birthday. I wrote "thank yous" to Oma and Aunt Natalie, plus Nicole Estes, a friend of Emilie's, who happened to be a nurse on the floor under the one Jacob was staying, Sharon Davidson, and several of Emilie's friends from her church in Boerne. Names I knew not. The following evening my second journal entry was even shorter: **"Thursday"**

Not only is it the 8th day since Jake's big diagnosis, but it was also my last day at Wave's Z's. I tried my best to focus at the task at hand, but my mind was not in the leasing paper work, or even in College Station. I checked my cell phone every 10 minutes to keep up with Jake. I knew my Dad was texting the updates because of his word choice, "Big Jake's white blood cell counts are down just a few ticks to 2,300. His platelet count is in the 30's." I read the last text several times. I asked the same question each time, why aren't his platelets increasing? The next text read, "Platelet transfusions were on the immediate agenda. His platelet counts have to be in the 50 plus range before the surgeons can perform surgery." "Surgery?" My text responses were a little less wordy. Things at the hospital picked up, so Dad didn't respond to my question. I was thankful for Caring Bridge at that precise moment, because of the positive encouragement posted: "Emilie spent time with Jacob by playing games and the like. Jake laughed and was amused just like the Jake we know." Though it was short and sweet, that was enough for me to go about my day with less of a heavy heart.

CHAPTER 11

On September 17th, Doctor Geo called it
"Surgery Day" having been pleased with the small
spike in Jake's platelet the night before. On Thursday
night, he had already planned and prepared for a
busy Friday for Jake starting at 1:30PM. He was due
for another spinal tap plus the drawing of bone
marrow from his hip to see if the chemo is working to
Big Jake's advantage. After he recovered from that,
on the same day, the Doctor would do the surgery.

The installation of a "portacath" in Jake's chest,
right below his left pectoral muscle, required an
extremely careful surgery because it would be placed
so near to Jacob's heart.

Once the boys were released from school, they
traveled with Dad to the hospital. They wanted to be
there when Jacob woke up from recovery before they
headed for College Station in time for Jeb's Aggie ring
ceremony the next day. As they waited for him to
wake up, the anesthesiologist even commented on
how polite Jacob was through the whole thing. She
added that she even thought he was the most polite

boy she has ever met. Drugged or not drugged.

Since the portacath was the pathway through which Jake would receive Chemotherapy, the Doctors removed the IV from his arm after they knew there were no complications with the "port" in Jake's chest. With the specific surgeries, Jacob also received another dose of chemo. It was late afternoon when Jake finally came to from his procedures. Dad stood next to him, so he would see a familiar face,

"Hey Jake, I am here with you."

Jake, still "doped up" replied with a smile, "Awe, cool Dad... is the thing in my chest?" (speaking of the portacath).

Dad answered, "yes, Son. It is."

Jake smiled again, "awe, cool." Having never been put under before; Dad said it was really funny to see his facial expressions. The boys, and Emilie got to see Jacob after the surgery. They all laughed when the nurses gave him something to drink and it came with a bendy straw. Jake's reply was with the famous, and none-other, "awww! It is a bendy straw!! His excitement proceeded with amazement over how it bent so many different ways.

Emilie, Dad and the boys left Mom and Jacob reluctantly to get sleep for the night before they were to travel another three hours to College Station on Saturday. We actually had planned this event since the beginning of August. Everyone was to come to the ceremony and celebrate after; then we'd all go to the Aggie versus Florida International game on Saturday. Jeb bought a total of 13 tickets in October and "kept them safe" as he explains, but since Jacob's diagnosis one could guess the many alterations to our plans.

I was the only family member able to make Justin Junior's ceremony. We decided to walk, all dressed up, from his house to the Clayton W. Williams Jr. alumni center. We had to wait outside in the heat, both of us were sweating bead by bead yet my brother's huge smile never left his face.

Finally, dressed in maroon and white, the line shortened, and we were indoors now. Jeb asked that I present his ring to him just seconds before I had time to process the honor it was. One of the Alumni in the B section took one "goofy picture" and one "precious moment" picture probably assuming we were a couple, as many people did. As we stepped outside, Jeb was greeted by some of our good friends with their congratulations. He seemed to feel special, but I could tell he missed the rest of the family and his girlfriend, Katherine.

Upon the family's arrival, we all met at a Mexican restaurant in downtown Bryan which is highly normal as our entire family qualifies chips and salsa as a main food group. Even Hillary traveled six hours by herself to offer her congratulations to our big brother. The apartments at which Jeb and I worked gave a huge discount to my family, so they could have a comfortable place to stay. Jeb and Emilie dunked their Aggie rings together later on that night. Dad had to finish Emilie's pitcher for her because she could not get past the gag reflex of lukewarm-cheap beer suds. Jeb finished his in a record time of: "very slow and did not feel well afterwards". He agreed that that Aggie tradition was not as fun as it looked.

Uncle Sam, Mom's brother younger by 20 years, and his wife Jessica, drove in from Edna for the game on Saturday just in time to eat lunch with us. Though it was easy to get caught in the excitement around us, part of our hearts yearned for Jake and Mom. Shortly after lunch, we stood outside the restaurant, hot and full, figuring the best ways to caravan and park near Kyle field when Dad's phone rang… always so loudly. His eyes lit up when finding it to be his wife, and his entire posture straightened as he listened to what was said on the other end!

"That is fantastic news! Alright! Yea, hold on. Hey, kids, Jake is being released from the hospital! His counts are going up, and the doctors are pleased. He has to stay close though…" Before he could finish, Emilie blurted out, "They can stay with me! I'll meet them there! But I need a car." And without missing a beat, Jeb now blurted out, "you can take the ol Jetta, Em." Handing her the keys at the same moment.

Upon arriving home, Emilie's district mentor, Kathy Williams, had supper ready for the eating. Because discharging can take a few hours, Mom and Jake arrived just in time to share the hot meal.

Hours away, yet at the same time, the rest of us forced ourselves into the Aggie spirit and waved the towels, shouted "AAAAAAAAAAAAAAA" and sang the Aggie War Hymn four or five times, and swayed our way into the next day.

I was so very anxious to get home and help out in all the ways I figured I could. With my brother's and Dad's help, we loaded my stuff into the trailer hitched to the suburban in just under an hour.

It started to rain just seconds after loading the last box. Dad and Elliot were in the car ahead pulling the load full of my belongings. Garrett and I followed in my car, trunk and back seat full as well. Garrett was always a happy passenger and I was grateful I didn't have to drive alone. He asked me shortly after our farewells to Jeb and Katherine if I was going to miss College Station.

I didn't know if I was going to or not. Getting home seemed more important than leaving my job, friends, church and school behind. I wanted to say yes, but at that moment, I didn't feel like I would.

Instead I said, "I will miss Jeb and Katherine and those calm nights at his house on Fairview, drinking hot chocolate and watching the Office instead of doing homework."

I was glad the two of them had each other. Jeb was so close to graduating that he too was ready to leave College Station for good.

The trip home was the first time I had spent four, uninterrupted hours with Garrett. I got to know how he thought and what he wondered. He, I always knew, was very sympathetic, but what I didn't realize is that he had the same fears and worries, as I. Garrett told me that he felt guilty for the way he treated Jacob the morning of his diagnosis. Garrett wasn't rude, but he didn't pay attention to Jacob at all. He said he went about his morning routine, executing his chores quickly so he could get a bowl of cereal in his stomach before Dad took them to school that morning.

Watching the road intensely, gripping the steering wheel as if to hold on for more control of the car, the rain and wet roads reminded me of September ninth. I told Garrett that placing blame on others and even ourselves is human nature, but that it isn't healthy. All we can do now is to offer Jacob love and support.

As we moved swiftly across the damp roads, our conversations went swiftly from school to sports to dreams and ambitions. It was encouraging to hear Garrett's raw desires straight from his heart, without any shame to quiet them.

Chapter 12

Emilie was a perfect comfort for Jacob's semi-outpatient time. She offered just the right amount of goofiness and love, so Jacob got a little taste of home. Jeb mailed The Office series which consisted, then, of a total of five seasons. Emilie thought this would hold Jake over for a couple of months, but to all of our surprise, he finished all the seasons in a matter of weeks. Emilie didn't catch on to the humor of the show like Jacob, but hearing him laugh, she explained, was the greatest joy yet.

Nose bleeds seemed to be the one thing to watch out for, and of course, fever over 100.5 degrees Fahrenheit. I called Emilie, Sunday evening, to see how Jacob was doing. She said that they went out Sunday afternoon to get some fresh air. It was really cool and breezy, but they went out to River Road Park where the enjoyed feeding the ducks and fish. They said they were able to walk around for a little while until Jake started feeling tired. When they got back to the house, Emilie and Jake had a pretty good scare. The "port" in his chest really started to bother him. Emilie said that she called and talked to a couple of nurses and tried sounding calm, cool, and collected in front of Jacob, but deep down she feared for his life. It ended up that he was just having some post-operative pains and that was the most he had exerted himself in over a week. It was to be expected.

I started to get settled back home with Elliot, Garrett and Dad for good company. Mom drove in early that morning to do some work at the dental office and visit with the rest of the family. Only stopping for one meal with Oma and Opa, at our town's famous Willow Creek Café, she left for Boerne right after dinner with an envelope full of letters from Mrs. Lehmberg's 4th grade class.

We got to hear how much Jake really enjoyed reading them. He laughed at their cute way of spelling and the repetitive drawing of a football player with a number 44 on the front of the jersey.

That same evening, I wrote out a chart of all I needed to clean, move around, and make functional for Jake to have someone close to his room, and with a clean bathroom nearby. That task overwhelmed me, so I called my Aunt Natalie, the guru of organization and proper cleaning methods, and asked for her help. She agreed wholeheartedly.

The 11th day of Jacob's journey came with the results of his bone marrow and spinal fluid samples. Breaths were held as the revealed results showed his blasts (immature white cells) comprise 15 percent of the total marrow. If a sample had been taken when Jacob was admitted 11-days ago, the doctors suspected that total to be 90 percent or more, based upon his near 400,000 white blood cell count.

"If this percentage drops 10% more, Jacob will officially be in remission!" The doctor re-stated this with more enthusiasm.

Praising the hard work of the doctors and staff of Methodist Children's Hospital, we grew ecstatic with the knowledge that Jacob's body was now slowly regenerating itself. It was also projected that Jake would be released to go home in as few as 5 -7 days.

Upon hearing this, our family and whole town buzzed with hope and joy.

Even after 11 days of suffering from nausea spells, nose bleeds, and aches, he was determined to keep it from taking control of his mind and spirit. It was hard not to fixate on his weight loss. In such a short amount of time, he was down to about 200 lbs. At the beginning of football season, he weighed 228 pounds. We were told that this was to be expected, unfortunately.

Aunt Natalie and I cleaned like crazy maids awaiting the Queens arrival. We steamed the carpet, scrubbed the walls, rearranged Jacob's room, washed the baseboards, scrubbed the pseudo- tile floors, dusted, vacuumed, and sterilized all the silverware. After all was said and done, it turned out to be a two-day project. I enjoyed having something to do, to be contributing. Cleaning the house was usually always my job, and to be doing something familiar made me feel more connected to the whole situation, yet, when time grew closer for Jake to return, I doubted it was sterile enough, so I cleaned again.

The word spread quickly how crucial it was to keep Jake quarantined. I feared this would offend people, but they continued to surprise me. Every day since the diagnosis, at one point or another, families from our community brought us meals, pies, cookies, cakes and money. Each person so considerate and genuine; it impressed me how everyone seemed to know how to act, or what to say. The town didn't line up at the door, intrude or become too pushy. Instead they went through Aunt Natalie. She designated herself secretary of the meal committee. Everyone called her to schedule times they would make dinner or dessert, and Aunt Natalie or Oma would hand deliver. Aunt Nat described the system as fun, but that it was also a way she felt connected too.

So many wanted to help in some way; and in so many ways, help appeared. It trickled in with different flavors and texture; encompassed our senses of smell with tasteful aroma, it tugged on our hearts with words of encouragement, and acts of kindness. It even came in the form of laughter, tears and solemn silence.

That following Wednesday, I arrived in Boerne around 9:15 AM. Big Jake was still asleep, and Mom seemed to be enjoying the quiet time. Suffering seemed to disappear when Jake slept. That peace was always welcome. We woke Jake shortly after my arrival, and he greeted me with a smile. He was ready for breakfast and asked specifically for biscuits, sausage and gravy. (One of Mom's specialties). His stomach was a little weak the day before, so extreme caution was added to the recipe. Three loaded biscuits down, and four more with grape jelly to go, Jake looked satisfied.

Boy, was his appetite recognizable!

After breakfast I showed him his surprise!

In the midst of my honorary discharge from my commitments in College Station, I had asked a few residents to whom I had sold their apartments for a favor. Two were on the Aggie basketball team. They were able to get a basketball and had their teammates sign it, as well as allowing me to photograph them holding a huge poster with the words: Play For Jake. My co-workers had worked overnight to orchestrate such an opportunity.

Jake's reaction was well worth every awkward conversation and request leading up to his gift. "Oh my gosh, oh my gosh! They did this for me? Oh wow!" I poured Jacob more milk as we continued discussing the excitement. "I keep getting a sense of God's love, and it never seems to stop!" Jake's voice cracked as he said this.

Upon hearing these words, I couldn't help but smile. Jake is God's son, and everything IS going to be okay. Thanks to the Aggie men's basketball team, we were reminded of His promise!

Just minutes later, our excitement was interrupted by Jake's urge to vomit. Uncertain at how this would play out, I was relieved to find it was just a bad taste in his mouth from all the acidic build up in his stomach.

He tried to get it out by forcing a deep cough, but this was counteracted with a sharp pain in his chest, taking over the urge to vomit. Mom handed him some Zofran, which really seemed to help him keep back the reflux and sharp pains. I was grateful to see the sudden relaxation in Jacob's face. The acidic build up, though, was still strong. Milk seemed to be the only thing that would calm it down, so he drank half a gallon of that, one cup full at a time.

"Since the milk feels really good going down, I wish the milk could filter down my throat non- stop."

Feeling this to be a wonderful idea, we bounced thoughts off one another and decided on a milk candy that dissolved slowly as the most probable solution...

Meanwhile, Mom waited for our inventive minds to come back down to the room, "Jake, I want you to do at least one subject in school today."

The stack of homework seemed an impossible feat. Jake had a hard time sitting up for long periods of time, so we thought up another great idea. This one took action right away. One vocabulary quiz was on the agenda. As a studying method, I put the words on flash cards, and handed them to Jake to study. He knew every word back to front. He took his quiz with great aplomb... yes, that was one of the words... And one point goes to: Jess!

(Jake and I made up a game: for every vocabulary word used through-out the day, you get a point.) It started off with a dollar a word, but Jake kept using all the words, and I continued emptying my wallet... He felt bad, so we made it a point game instead.

We had so much fun being out of the school structure and making up our very own semi-efficient structure. Jake told me that the day was flying by, so he checked the time reading aloud, "2:30! We skipped lunch!" This instantly triggered an internal reminder that he was indeed hungry for lunch.

The hardest thing for Jake was coping with his lack of strength. He was so used to having such a busy schedule, slightly stressing about football practice, homework, chores...etc. When he would break into a sweat just walking down the hall to the restroom, he struggled accepting it. We agreed that the only way to overcome this was taking one step at a time. His merry heart worked just fine. At about 5:30 in the afternoon, Mom brought fried chicken and delicious Macaroni and Cheese from Kentucky Fried Chicken. Jake ate three huge chicken strips and three bowls of Mac and Cheese... Mom and I had our share too.

It was time for Mom to leave for Mason and take care of the other boys in her life: Dad, Elliot and Garrett. On the other end of things, they missed her a lot too. What a mother can endure is beyond me!

While we waited for Emilie to come home, Jake and I had fun visiting and listening to the sounds Emilie's house makes. When Em arrived, she brought a new energy for that night. We told her about our day, and she told us about hers. Quite eventful on both sides.

Shortly after all the pills had been swallowed, the yawns followed. We went to bed around 10:15. Before we prayed, Jake got our attention, "I am really grateful to both of you. I am so comfortable in your house, Em. I feel safe, secure and in God's hands, but I am ready to be home.

CHAPTER 13

Our minds and hearts anxiously awaited the moment we would know if Jacob would be in remission. Jake and I grabbed a few things, hopped in the car with Mom, and made it to his appointment with a few minutes to spare. I couldn't comprehend how Jacob did it: blood, needles, chemotherapy, bigger needles and more blood... I was restless in my seat watching the chemo travel slowly down the long thin tube towards Big Jake's heart. Jake noticed my discomfort and thought of a few ways to make me feel comfortable. Ironic, I know.

As we were sitting in the "Fish" room and staring at the chemo in silence, Jacob then started humming the theme song to "Jaws" faster and faster as the chemo got closer and closer to his chest. We couldn't help our laughing aloud, and the nurse opened the door really quickly to make sure everything was okay... We stopped abruptly while trying to look inconspicuous, but just as she shut the door behind her we continued to think we were just that, inconspicuous.

After Jake had his chemo, we walked down long cold hallways, took five left turns and one right turn and we were in the surgery area. It was time for Jake to get some of his bone marrow tested. We can always tell when we have new nurses because all their reactions are the same, "oh, he is a big kid."

If only they had seen him just two weeks prior.

Jacob was excited about the anesthesia. He smiled when he felt the sleep coming on. "I like that stuff. It makes me feel so comfortable," was mentioned quite often in the recovery room.

That only made one of us. Mom and I sat in the crowded waiting room and carried on a quiet conversation as if the other people would be bothered by our noise. The reports stated that his platelets were back to normal, and that is all on his own immune system. God continued to amaze me with his continued showering of grace. Yet, Jake was still losing weight. The second Friday after his diagnosis he was under 200lbs. His bruising was still very visible, and his once so defined muscle mass was starting to wither before our eyes.

After his long appointment, we found our way to the comfort of Emilie's home and put on a movie. Laying on the couch that night, Jacob continuously kept swinging his leg back and forth in quick motions. When I asked him what he was doing, "I'm looking for my calf muscle.... it seems to be missing. Have you seen it anywhere?"

I couldn't help but laugh at his reaction to losing his own muscles, but I felt so badly for him. I opened my mouth to offer words of encouragement like, "don't worry, it will come back soon enough" or "I still see some definition" but nothing seemed good enough. He looked so strong not even a month ago. I wanted to feel sorry for him all over again, but before I said anything, I knew Jake was not going to give up. He knew he could control one thing, and that was what he consumed for his body. He drank half a gallon of milk almost every day thinking of his bones. He ate like Sam Wise, our favorite Hobbit from the Shire in the "Lord of the Rings" series, hoping his strength would return. He didn't focus on his physical changes entirely, and instead thanked God for sparing his life. Instead of encouraging Jacob, I decided to tell him he was an encouragement to me.

"Thanks Jess. Could you make me my second lunch?" Spoken in character as Sam.

As I was making him his sandwich, I searched to see if he was maybe feeling sorry for himself to be missing yet another football game. "Are you sure you want me to go, tonight? I'd be really happy to play games here with you!"

Jacob put his pointed finger up in the air, perched his lips, and shook his head at my question, as though it was just plain nonsense.

"You're better at filming than Mom or Dad." Jake was in definite game mode. I drove home with the instructions Jacob gave me in honor of his buddies for Friday night. Meanwhile, Jake would watch Elliot and Garrett's football games prior to this week's with Emilie.

Once I arrived back in Mason, with just an hour before the game, I found Jake's "Fat Boy" shirt again. This Fat Boy shirt is a tradition the Linemen coach started Jake's freshmen year. All the linemen wore a solid purple shirt with white lettering, FAT BOYS, on game day. A unique bond went along with the wearing of this shirt, and Jacob wanted me to wear it once again, so his teammates knew he was thinking of them. Though I had eaten much more in the last few weeks, I still didn't fill this shirt out like Jacob once did, and I by no means felt worthy of this shirt. It was a connection that only they knew. As I was doing my hair in preparation for the football game, Dad called us all into the living room. His excitement beaming from his voice only meant one thing! I was grateful for the way Dad likes to explain news.

"We all can agree that the way God moves is mysterious indeed. If saints and song writers had not shared their gifts, it would be hard to express happiness. A favorite hymn of ours, gives us just the right words, "Praise God from whom all blessings flow, praise Him all creatures here below, praise Him above ye heavenly host, praise Father, Son and Holy Ghost…" Dad took a deep breath and continued,

"The technical aspects of his bone marrow and platelet counts are beyond my capability to comprehend. As I understand it, normal folks do have about five percent of these blast cells in their bone marrow. When someone's counts go above five percent, they have leukemia. Jacob's percentage of blast cells is at one percent! In fact, a different, more sensitive test reveals the count is at 0.3 percent. Based upon his platelet counts at 146 from earlier today, means that Jacob's immune-recovery system is regenerating on its own! Because of God's work and grace, our Jacob is in remission!"

Dad choked up with gratitude and amazement. My eyes filled with tears for the first time in a while with overwhelming joy.

Jacob doesn't have cancer anymore! Joy expressed through laughter filled our small home as Dad continued, "Dr. Geo also conferred with his associates in Houston and based upon their research of children who exhibit this kind of turn-around, Jacob can be considered well on his way to full recovery. We still have a long way to go, but the demonstration of God's grace is so overwhelming, I cannot begin to describe it. We will get to welcome Jacob home on Sunday!"

It would be impossible even to begin to express how we all felt. Hugs and kisses were passed between us at home, and even when we sat in the reserved box seat at the football field, Puncher Dome. I watched anxiously as the game went on and we streaked by with a victory.

My mind, though, was not on the game. I was still in question. I know I wasn't the only one who, in the deepest part of our hearts, still thought that this was too good to be true. Of course, I thanked God. Everyone began to breathe again. Jacob didn't have Leukemia anymore... but that didn't necessarily mean that it was all over.

CHAPTER 14

I put pen to paper, again, as I tried to process the wonderful news. Friends and the community started making signs for welcoming Jacob home and placing them alongside the highway, leading to our front steps. I was so glad he was finally coming home. He would get to sleep in his own bed, put his suitcase under his bed and use his dresser again... I still felt ill-equipped to take care of him. My mind went from one thing to another. I couldn't help but wonder if he could skip the chemotherapy since his body was reacting well anyway. I hoped that this could be possible. Why was chemo necessary? It is poison.

Yet, God had a different plan.

The day after the football game, Elliot and I moved his and Garrett's beds, dressers and clothes to the back room, so Jacob could have the room next to mine. We thought it better that Jacob and I share the bathroom in between our rooms... I am proud to say I am much cleaner than 15 and 13-year-old boys. I started to feel more at ease with the house clean, again. Jacob was to be home mid-afternoon that Sunday.

Elliot and Dad went to Boerne to pick up Jacob and Mom from Emilie's house. Before heading out, they did some yard work as Emilie had neglected her lawn to give her full attention to the family. Dad was concerned she would be fined for unruly grass. Jacob watched, laughing at the different activities, but was eager to get home.

Finally, Garrett and I ran out to meet Jacob. He told us later that he missed everything so much, that he even missed the smell of our neighbor's cow manure.

Jacob's condition still seemed too scary. We were afraid to touch him or anything he might use. Mom and I washed dishes on the highest pressure in the dishwasher; we had Lysol spray in every corner. Jacob had Lysol wipes and hand sanitizer within an arm's length. The boys no longer spent all their extra time at their friend's houses for fear of accumulating more germs.

If visitors came, we had them come in the back door, so they could remove their shoes and pass through the disinfectant process. The Mason community was very considerate of our worries and concerns and kept their children at a distance from Jacob with his susceptible condition. What impressed me and even humbled me more was that after a month into the new life style, we were still receiving meals almost every night.

Weber's Chevron gas station took up forces with the Mason Cancer Society and gave us free gas for our trips to the clinic or hospital in San Antonio.

Jacob's chemotherapy still left an aching sting in my heart.

Why did it have to be this way?

Jacob had been checking in at the clinic every Friday for two weeks now. It helped so much having help with gas cost. The owners even recognized which cars were ours and would have the receipt ready for signing right after we'd fill up. They send us off with a smile, "have a good one."

I went with Jacob and Mom the second time to the clinic. Jacob felt nauseated the whole way to San Antonio. Once we arrived, the receptionist behind the glass room recognized Jacob and handed him the yellow bracelet with the barcode. Mom signed some papers and they instantly led us through the double doors. They weighed and measured Jacob. It was quite funny seeing the barely five-foot male nurse, Charles, stand on his very tip toes to get the measuring bar above Jacob's head.

The things required of Jacob's five phase recovery seemed more achievable having support from all aspects of life. I rested well at night, and I knew Mom and Dad were beginning to as well.

Phase one was a great learning phase. It required chemotherapy once a week. We went Fridays; because that was the day Mom was off from work. We got to know the staff better, and better understood everything that was tested for and the reason for everything…

Prevention.

With Big Jake home, we were already in need of some groceries. I don't think I can say this enough, "This boy can eat!"

Our wonderful friends had brought us so many dinners that we laid out all the food buffet-style. The idea was to pick which meal you wanted, and it would be heated. Well, that was not the case for Jake. There was no "pick which" but there was a "pick each" for our Big Jake. He had everything on the menu.

We were so grateful his eating was back to normal, that no-one said anything about the mountain of food on his plate.

This energy source resulted in positive progress for Big Jake. As the days and nights went by, Jacob stayed motivated. He continued to impress Mom and me as he tackled his History homework without being told. Although, when we told him to do his Algebra homework, we received a whole new reaction.

While Jake was studying with little to no help from me, Mom stayed in the kitchen preparing breakfast for the days she'd be going back to work full time. Her boss gave her another week off to recover from the weeks prior. I was grateful for her being around, because I still felt unprepared for being responsible for my little brother. It was encouraging to be near Jake as he felt so good. He even told me he wanted to knock out all his homework from the two weeks prior. I was glad he felt well enough to do that, because THAT WAS A LOT OF HOMEWORK!

Diligently pouring over his homework, stretching his mind, resulted in a negative push back from his body. Instead of just black ink across his paper, red drips trickled on it, and before he could keep more from ruining his work, a puddle had formed, with more spilling over his lips, and hands to his elbows, on the table, chairs and floor.

Mom and I acted fast. She grabbed a damp towel, and I grabbed his homework to try to save what was left, cleaning up all around him. Jake tilted his head back trying to stop its flow.

Quickly glancing at the clock, I counted in my head when this must stop before we'd have to rush to San Antonio. Fifteen minutes on the grand scheme of things, really isn't that long, yet this particular 15 minutes felt like 15 hours. I wasn't quite sure if I had ever seen that much blood. Little to my knowledge, in two months I would report that much blood as nothing compared to a future incident.

If a nosebleed lasted longer than ten minutes we were instructed to call the doctor. Mom did not wait the full ten and called with just five minutes down.

With Dr. Geo's instructions and with some prayer and devotion, in the remaining minutes, it finally clotted. Mom, Jake and I sighed at the exact same moment.

After a little rest, Jake started back and finished his English homework. The final assignment for English required a reading of <u>Plymouth</u> <u>Plantation</u>. Jake pronounces it: "ply-mouth." He started reading out loud in an English accent but then the old English words kind of messed up his rhythm, so he ended up reading to himself...

CHAPTER 15

Loneliness really hadn't hit Jacob quite yet. He mentioned once or twice that he missed his friends but didn't make too big a deal out of it. I keep thinking if it had been me, I'd be either on my phone or begging for visitors... not Jacob.

I learned quickly to notice the small things that Jacob was able to do. Mid-afternoon usually marked the peak of Jake's wellness. He had a sudden burst of energy, sat up from the sofa, "Do y'all want to go outside? I'd like to ride the bike."

Stopping whatever it was we were doing, we laced up and followed him outside. Mom and I felt the same "wonderfulness" of Wednesday, and immediately encouraged him, frankly because it encouraged us.

Jake did ride his bike... up the 300-meter street, then back down the street... then back up, then back down. He continued this repetitive expedition about five or six times.

After his ride, we all sat in lawn chairs and admired the day. Charlie was glad to have visitors, so she stopped by for free pettings one by one. Mom waited for Jake to catch his breath, "Someone is turning 17 in just a few days."

"Oh, that's right, Jake, you got any big plans?" I felt it appropriate to joke.

"I was planning on throwing a keg party with just a few of my close friends... Y'all can come too if ya want." Our laughter was cut short when Jake's nose started to bleed. Thankfully, it was controllable, and only lasted about three minutes. While Jake was pinching the bridge of his nose he peeked around his fingers at me, "you know, I love the smell of the country air."

I thought he was going to describe the fresh cut grass, or the sunflowers and maybe even the slightly damp sand... NOPE!

"I thought this when we drove up when I came home from the hospital, but the old cow manure really smells like home... And it is so peaceful out here."

"I think only born farmers and ranchers can agree with you on that one... and maybe Emilie."

The next day, Jake's joints began to ache, a side effect from the medications, so he had not rested well the night before. It was the first time I'd witness him become grumpy in 27 days. He walked back and forth in the kitchen without saying anything. Repeated this motion three or four times and finally exclaimed, "My jaw is tight; my stomach hurts and I think I am in a bad mood."

Not having a good response, I instead played some music. Jake loves music, something he inherited from Dad. The "Rocky" theme song penetrated the walls of our home. Jake fought back a smile, took a shower, blended some raw eggs and milk together and became a new man…. Or he just took a shower and came out of it a little happier. He read a chapter in his history book and set up skype. Since algebra and chemistry were too difficult to self-teach, the school made it possible for him to join in real time for his classes. Jake started feeling less cranky but felt lightheaded if he stood up for too long. He had hopes to ride his bike again but postponed it just one more day.

His body started to puff up, unrelated to the carbs and proteins consumed and more because of the large dosage of Prednisone he was regimented. Instead of groaning about his new look, he made his lips very small, and said, "I'm Russel from "Up", now."

That day it seemed as though nothing was really wrong, and that the near future was going to be very doable. Jacob woke up each day ready to conquer. He agreed to be placed into a study protocol with the hopes that someone else would benefit from the study results just as he has thus far. The end of Mom's week free from work was near the end. Jacob was to receive his last chemo treatment in the IV form that Friday in San Antonio and begin Phase 2.

He spent his entire birthday day at the clinic hooked up to IVs, learning of the next four phases with Mom and Dad. They all listened intently as the oncologist explained the treatment to come:

"Jacob responded very well to the induction phase, phase one, attaining remission. No leukemia cells are present in his bone marrow or spinal fluid. However, his WBC is down to 4,100 and his platelets are low at 97. It is expected for these counts to fluctuate as the residual effects of chemo continue to flow through Jacob's body. This next phase is called consolidation. It will last about 2 months. We also call it the knock-out-punch." He continued to explain that decades ago, once in remission, doctors thought that the patient was cured, yet patients would return in three or four months with relapse of leukemia. This consolidation and the phases following have been developed over the last 60 years of research and that is why the treatment success for Jacob's type of leukemia (T-cell ALL) has gone from 5% to 85%.

"So, is this phase two?" Jake picked up one of the IV tubes.

"Well, partially. You will still be receiving some of the same drugs, plus some. Research has shown that leukemia cells can become resistant to chemo. These new drugs will be given to prevent resistance. At the same time, you will be receiving regularly large doses, weekly, of fluids and electrolytes to protect your kidneys and bladder. Are you ready for your LP?"

Jake winced at the thought of it… this was the only procedure that caused any form of anxiety.

Responding as doctors do, he gave him 2 mg of a drug, slowly pressing the plastic syringe into the connection tubes, "this will help you relax, Buddy."

"Is it the same feeling of being stoned? I wouldn't know."

Smiles surfaced and within minutes, he was completely relaxed.

"Are you all stoning me?" with a bigger grin now, he looked at the nurse and exclaimed, "wow, you have four eyes and two noses!"

Mom was then taught how to administer Jacob's medications through his port. If she was nervous, she did not show it. Having wanted to be a nurse her whole life, she seemed to be in a good place.

With the okay from the doctor, Jake was allowed to attend that night's football game, with the instructions of staying in the open air, away from the crowd. Luckily, it was a home game, and the arrangements could be made by our dear friends, the Hofmans, whose eldest son, Dyllan was Jacob's best friend since grade school. No day went by that Jake did not hear from Dyllan.

Our beloved Punchers won 40-6 over the Eagles of Eldorado. His teammates traditionally face the band at the end of the game while the band plays the Puncher school song. Instead, the team, cheerleaders and coaches turned and faced Jacob who was standing on the Northwest corner of the field. Jake's favorite birthday present was standing yards away in front of him. Tears rolled down his cheek as his gleaming grin shined back at his brothers.

Trying not to feel sorry for his son, Dad couldn't help but feel a sense of how desperately Jake wanted to suit up and resume playing ball again.

Yet, never once did Jake complain.

CHAPTER 16

I look back now at how quiet and peaceful that day was, out in the sun, watching Jake trek a few yards back and forth on the too small bike... I remember grinding my teeth and praying for that day to return.

Phase two hit Jacob like an oversized sledge hammer to the body. We were not prepared or anywhere near ready for this type of illness. I feel as though my writing will not do justice to the horrible condition Jacob was in. I wrote more during the second month than any. I cried and prayed for the instant I could say, "it is behind us now." Though a rough memory, it is now only a memory.

When Jacob woke up in the morning, he threw up, when he stood up to use the restroom, he threw up, when he took a shower, he'd get a bloody nose, and then throw up. His "hobbit" appetite shifted to that of a teething baby. Jacob ate popsicles and drank popsicles. That is all he had the strength to hold up to his mouth and keep down for the few hours his body allowed him.

This phase is considered the Knock Out phase because he received chemo in several different forms almost every day. That last Friday of Phase one, they accessed his portacath so we could induce the chemo at home. The doctors call this Ara- C. The only good thing about that, was the fact that we were saving gas, but inputting chemo, personally was hard on Mom and me.

For her lunch break, Mom came home to start the process. I found some fun in wearing the latex gloves, and distracting Jacob, as I timed the accessing Mom had to do. It started with a saline flush. This step seemed innocuous as the liquid was clear like water. Mom had to test to see if it was going the right route by drawing back a couple of millimeters of blood, then returning it. If blood did not return, something was wrong. I found that we all held our breath during this time. Mom then had to give the 15 millimeters of chemo. The bag was "caution" taped and had the hazardous sign in a huge and bold illustration on the front and back of the bag. This had to be admitted slowly, in a time span of 1 to 2 minutes.

After the last millimeter, she then flushed the accessed port with Heparin. My job was to hand Mom the syringes, alcohol wipes and make sure the bucket was near. I was glad my job was simple. I couldn't even begin to know how it would feel being responsible for a treatment as crucial as this. Jacob was so calm and trusting staying still and strong while Mom acted doctor.

Mom prayed aloud each time this was to be done, "Lord, guide my hand and make the chemo work for good in Jacob's body and not for bad. Thank you for your grace and mercy." Her eyes barely blinking until the process was complete.

Jacob, unfortunately was able to smell the liquid, Heparin which made him queasy. Jake's doctor warned him that he would either taste it or smell it, but either way, it would not settle well with his insides. He had to hold out until the final flush of saline to throw up.

On top of all that, he still had to take a chemo dose in pill form called, Mercaptopurine. And a pill called Bactrim, which is a sulfa drug that eliminates bacteria that causes infections. In other words, it is an antibiotic which makes Jacob very susceptible to 2nd degree sunburn. Jake was already fair skinned, so sunscreen in the winter time was not that unusual. The only medicine he didn't mind was the serotonin blocker, Zofran. This nausea preventer is supposed to work as a receptor antagonist, yet three out of five days it would not work.

Each time after the first Ara-C done at home, Mom prayed the same prayer. Though her trust was in the Lord, Mom still felt an overwhelming pressure. One night at the dinner table, Mom dropped her fork and held her hand, as calm as someone can do when in pain.

"Honey, what's wrong?" Dad, always concerned for his bride.

"My hand just…. It's fine… there was a stabbing pain then I couldn't move it for a minute. It's okay now." At times the pain would be so bad she would have to ice it right then and there. We never understood why she felt this pain. We tossed around the idea that it was the beginning signs of carpel tunnel, (yet once the Knock Out phase ended, and the pain dissipated, we assumed it was stressed induced from the burden of administering chemo to her son).

This particular phase, Knock Out, was not only hard on Jacob physically and emotionally, but it also started testing me as well. I hate feeling helpless at any time, and I felt helpless all the time. Every day, I dumped his vomit bowl, rinsed it out, and sprayed it down with Lysol. Every day, I watched as he grew weaker and paler. Every day, he would lie in the same position and try and move as little as possible.

Late October, early morning I asked Jake if he'd like some eggs and bacon. He answered with a sharp, "NO."

"Would you prefer cereal, then?"

"NO."

"A piece of toast?"

"NO, Jessica. NO!"

"Wow, okay, I was just trying to help. What do you want?" I failed at hiding my offense.

"Nothing, Jess, because today, I feel like pound sign, question mark, star, exclamation point."

Despite his nausea ad nauseum he still found a way to make me smile, with the help of Kevin Fowler's G rated version for describing poop.

This quickly became a theme. Aches and pains kept him in a constant uncomfortable state. Standing or sitting up caused severe dizziness, lying flat on his back caused sharp pains down his neck, turning to the side caused projectile vomiting. Yet, he refused to be coddled for as long as possible. He was determined to get his own drinks of water, or snack from the kitchen. In the afternoon, we'd both be anxious for everyone to get home as sitting in silence became daunting and sad, despite my effort to lighten it up.

"I am really thirsty. "Jake stated this after I had just replaced his bowl emptied of vomit by his side.

"I'll get you some ice chips." Grateful to do something that didn't involve the dropping of contents in a toilet bowl.

"No, I'll get it, thanks." Yet he still laid there.

And continued to lie there. No movement.

I watched him for about two minutes.

"Are you sure, Buddy? My schedule is clear, I have time."

One more minute passed, I returned to the mystery I was holding in hand, trying to pick up where I left off, then I heard music, starting off slow and quiet, then growing louder and more intense. He had clicked on the "Chariots of Fire" ring tone on his cell phone and moved with the slow-paced beat to complete this task.

I silently cheered from the sideline, raising my hands like he was Eric Little finishing first and I, a worthy spectator.

No words were said, just music and small, slow motions.

Shortly after, Mom returned home, and gave all her attention to Jacob. Tending to him, finding new ways to suggest comfort and hope. Dad filtered in after picking up the two boys from practice. He was recommending they finish their homework before dinner and then we could all watch a program. There was little retort, and the house fell quiet again.

Mom prepared dinner, Dad sat in his chair reading, as I too tried finishing the pages in my hand. The boys scratched at their homework, writing fiercely to finish faster than the other. Everyone knew now Jake was becoming too weak to carry on conversation, but always wanted to be a part of what was going on in the Bibb living space.

Just a few minutes into dinner, Jacob's movement on the couch grabbed all our attention. He had to get up to relieve himself, one of the tasks we could not do for him. Trying to give Jake space, we, at the dinner table, returned to our food. Before sitting up completely, the silence broke with the "Rocky" theme song. We all looked up again, confused, and now watching closely as to what Jake was doing. The boys had been on extra good behavior, trying to be quiet and calm the past several weeks, so as not to disturb Jake, so having something as random as "Rocky" play, grabbed their complete attention.

Slowly, Jake sat up, stood up and took the few steps leading to the bathroom. Before entering, he raised his hands as Sylvester Stallone did when stepping up the final step of the long, steep staircase.

Elliot and Garrett looked at each other first with big grins, no words exchanged, filled with deep joy to witness Jake express his personality in such a way. Simultaneously, they cheered, applauding Jacob's success.

On Friday morning, we learned Jake's hemoglobin counts were extremely low putting him in the anemic category. Dehydration set in due to the few ice chips he could barely keep down. Though this was helpful in explaining why he felt so low on energy, we were definitely caught off guard when the doctors ordered IV fluids and a transfusion.

It was incredible watching color come to his face within just a few hours. The doctor suggested he take a little break from the amount of chemo he'd been receiving. Instead, he received two units of blood. Jake's bounce returned, and he mentioned for the first time that day that he'd like to attend the football game. No motivational music required.

That night, Hillary met us in Goldthwaite. Jake was especially excited to see her. Though we were isolated from the crowd, we were made to feel a big part of the evening. It was related to us that the Goldthwaite school had a check for Jake and would need family members to accept it on the field. Dad, Hillary and I agreed to the terms, and met the student council representative with the principal down on the field. Unknown to us, all that day the middle school and high school had a "hats off" day raising money to help support Jake's medical expenses. The entire Goldthwaite football team took their helmets off and stood respectfully during the presentation. Dad said in that moment, "that kind of character is what champions are made of."

To say we were humbled and blessed by this kindness and generosity is an understatement. I felt totally unqualified to be standing in the middle of that football field.

We watched, set apart, yet feeling so near, as the Punchers lost their first game.

The weekend was calm and enjoyable but looming over our heads was the upcoming appointment on Tuesday. We knew the doctors wanted him back on track receiving heavy dosages of chemo to continue to destroy those hidden blast cells.

The drive home was long. Nausea returned almost immediately, as if to say, "hey host, remember me?"

The days grew longer, and it was harder to find joy in the small things. There were no bike rides, or random walks taken. I was so discouraged and dreaded getting up in the morning and couldn't believe my brother continued to get out of bed, despite knowing exactly what awaited him. It seemed to me the trials and discouragement would never end, and I began to believe it. Jacob couldn't tell me he was okay. He couldn't even tell me how I could help.

At first, I felt offended when Jacob would not respond to a question I asked or if he didn't smile when I thought I was being funny. It took me a little over a week to understand the constant pain and discomfort Jacob was in, and how much energy it took for him to muster up a sentence and even stretch a small smile.

There was one thing he managed to do well, and that was grunting. I knew Jacob well enough too, that open ended questions were better not in the picture, so we stuck with "yes or no" answers. It was quite easy to catch on to his language. One short grunt meant "yes" and the longer grunt meant "no". There was even a "hell no" grunt and that grunt was very easy to decipher. I called it our modern form of Morse Code.

Each morning I'd pray, "Lord, please let Jake feel well enough to ride the bike again."

The day would pass, followed by a long night of toilet entries.

I'd pray again, "Lord, help Jake feel good enough to laugh again."

Morning and night, no laughter.

"Lord, maybe even just a smile?"

When the boys came home from school, they too understood Jacob's discomfort. They left him alone and tried to be as quiet as possible. The popsicles and Sprite were designated to Jacob and

Jacob only. One little argument the boys got into before Mom came home from work was when Garrett took a green popsicle out of the freezer. As he tried eating it before we caught him, he experienced a" brain freeze". Elliot scolded him, "that's what you get for stealing Jacob's popsicle."

Garrett knew he was in the wrong and couldn't think of an excuse. At that same time, Mom came in and saw that Garrett had half a Popsicle left. Before she could get on to him, Jacob worked up enough energy to say, "it's fine, I don't like the green ones."

I laughed as Garrett's face went from absolute guilt to immediate relief. Mom caved in and agreed, "okay, y'all can eat the green ones, but leave the rest for Jacob."

Through this whole argument, I acted like I was reading my book. It was nice to witness a little excitement in our dull day. Even though Jacob couldn't show it, I knew he appreciated it as well.

Mom stayed home with Jacob on most of Elliot and Garrett's game days, so I could have a break from the daily drain of poor Jacob's ailments. It was nice spending time with Dad and the other parents whose boys were on my little brother's teams.

I enjoyed the conversations between the mothers and fathers and was grateful they accepted me into every conversation. I knew all the town gossip in just one night's game. I don't count this as a successful goal, but it was something different than vomit, diarrhea and blood and I counted it as way too enjoyable. My aunt encouraged me to come to the weight- lifting class her church held every Monday, Wednesday and Friday. I was reluctant at first but decided it would be a good for me... and Jacob too. It was indeed. After the first class, I didn't feel like the walls were closing in on me. This encouraged me to keep going, and I did.

Jacob gave me one short grunt and that meant he too enjoyed the hour alone, without me breathing down his neck. He didn't "grunt" the last part, but then again, he didn't have too.

I felt like the original Cinderella. I vacuumed, mopped, dusted, washed dishes, cleaned the windows, our bathroom and did laundry every day. That kept me busy for the better part of the morning.

Since Jacob was too weak to do school work, we watched whatever "educational" show sparked our interest for that day. When he slept, I read. It was nice having time. I grew to enjoy it. I finished one book in a matter of a week-sometimes less. Some of the books started running together as I read them one after another. But the time engrossed in the pages was so nice. I did the cliché thing and imagined myself in China or wherever the pages took me.

I lost track of each hour, unlike a couple of months before. It seemed I would use an hour to plan the next hour, however, now, all Jacob and I could really do was wait for the next event. I at least could go out and be somewhat involved. Poor Jacob could barely move from the position from which he woke. Waiting always seems slower when your whole day is scheduled by it. Prisoners probably share this same thought.

The new thing besides the next episode of "Friends", was Hillary coming down to visit. The month of October seemed to drag on, so neither of us could wait for a different but very familiar face. Jacob tried hard to put on a happy face, but the effort wore him out. After Mom administered the chemo and we awed Hillary with the way we did things, Jacob held in his vomit as long as possible. The bowl was just out of his reach, but his projectile was just forceful enough that he managed to keep it all in the bowl. Hill jumped out of range and her awe became pity in a blink of an eye. Mom returned to work after emptying the bowl. I was glad not to have to do it. I wondered when vomit would not faze me anymore. Mom seemed able to ignore it.

The rest of the day was quiet, and I felt badly for Hill. She came to bring a new energy, but it didn't go far. Instead, she sunk into our daily routine. Once Jacob went to bed, Hill and I carried on a light conversation about her life. She said it was hard coming home because when she goes back to Abilene, everything she sees is a vague memory, and then she returns, and it hits her even harder. I tried telling her it was getting better, but really it was just the same and maybe even worse. In between our conversation, we heard Jacob get up and go to the bathroom over and over. He couldn't sleep. I left Hill to sleep on my bed and I took my pillow and sleeping bag to Jacob's floor. I felt the loneliness in his room even though it was decked out with banners signed by all his friends, letters and cards spread around the room from people in our community and surrounding communities and even the basketball signed by the Aggies. On his night-stand next to his "vomit-bowl" and Bible, cracked open with a pen, was his journal we'd given him at the very beginning of his treatment. We encouraged him to write his thoughts as they came to mind.

Desperate to know just how he felt, I quietly took his black journal from the stand, and used my cell phone as my light. Only one page was written on:

"My cup is overflowing, but God keeps pouring in His love"

-MY STORY-

A dream is the only way I can describe what I was feeling that day. My head was spinning as I laid there in the emergency room hearing the doctors explain my condition. I couldn't have given more of a blank stare when I heard the doctor say leukemia. "This is not real" was the only thought in my mind. I searched around the room looking for evidence that this is only a dream. Instead I saw my mom with tears rolling down her face and my dad clenching his jaw trying to fight back his. I finally felt the sting of reality. I finally saw how real this was. My mind started to cloud with fear and doubt. I felt like a lost abandoned boy weeping and begging for comfort. I cried out to the Lord, "God I need you. You are the Almighty and let your will be done and give me the strength to accept it."

At the point that I felt so lost and in need, I saw God do his amazing works. My older siblings who are spread out all over Texas dropped what they were doing and were there in a blink to see me. They came to the hospital and put a smile on my face. The next day I heard everyone in the community was praying and giving support. I saw how quickly and how great everyone responded to someone that was in need of love and I was amazed. God showed how great and amazing his love is through what my family, friends and community were doing for me. Then he helped me realize that I am only seeing the tip of the ice berg. I have not seen but a hint of God's unending love for his children. That lost abandoned boy who was crying and begging for comfort was picked up and embraced in welcoming arms. All fear and doubt were instantly swept away and replaced with comfort and strength.

The message I want to get across is that God will never leave his children. I know at times in our lives life just seems too much, and it is just you against the world and a sense of loneliness and fear starts to creep inside you. Well, all you have to do is realize that there is something a whole lot bigger than anything you're up against and He is on your side. The fear of abandonment and loneliness are two powerful forms of doubt that try to steer you away from God. They make you believe that you're alone and God is nowhere to be found when you're struggling, and this causes you to fall. But it is in these times of struggle, God is more evident than ever. You have fallen, and the Lord comes and picks you up and renews your strength that was drained from you by doubt. He gives you comfort when you were trembling and believing you were alone. He makes you realize that you were never alone and not for a moment had reason to fear. A while ago my dad shared a story about an old Indian ritual that made no connection to me until now. When a boy was to become a man, his father would take him out in the middle of the wilderness at night and blind fold his son. The son was instructed to sit on a stump and not to take off the blind fold until he felt the warmth of the sun on his face. The father would then leave, and the son would face the night hearing all the sounds of the wild and wonder what his fate would be out here by himself. He was left to wonder if he would be attacked and killed that night or make it to morning. And when the warmth of the sun's rays was felt the son would lift the blind fold to see his father watching over him and standing guard and the son realizes that he wasn't alone during the night that he had someone there protecting him. That realization is what I felt when I saw God's works of grace. At the time when I felt so alone and afraid, I realized that God was always with me and I never had reason to fear. No matter what your struggle is do not let fear and doubt cloud your mind for

God is with you and His amazing love and mercy will not let anything take you away from Him.

I looked around the room again, and despite all the color and well-wishing, it felt like a prison. Yet, although Jake was trapped inside a sick body, his hope was unchained. I wanted to feel that same hope.

Chapter 17

Feeling less helpful every day, my light-hearted attitude was nowhere to be found. I started contemplating my value as a care-giver and couldn't help but compare my lack of achievement to my peers. Living in a small town of just over 2000 residents, I half expected everyone to know why I was not attending college. I had been back at home for over a month now and I know how fast news travels, but still I was asked in the Mexican restaurant for which I used to waitress, "why aren't you in school?"

And I was asked in our only grocery store, "I see you around a lot, where are you going to school?"

And also, at the post office, our town square, movie theatre, same questions. I answered the same way every time, and it even sounded rehearsed to me, "I moved home to help my family out."

And then it would happen, the look of sympathy and pity all in one glance. I grew annoyed by this look. It only lifted the pedestal people put me on. It felt like an excuse. Because of this, it made me feel guilty. Guilty for the times I became angry or irritated for being home. I caught myself dusting where I had already dusted to somehow prove my purpose. Unsure how to express my frustrations, and definitely not wanting anyone to know I had second thoughts, I wrote down everything in a messy hurry:

"Life moving on without me seems unfair. I am officially behind and will probably never catch up to my peers. If I return to school in 1 year, I will have 2 more remaining. I will be older than Emilie was when she graduated from college. Hillary will have finished before me. I hate this feeling. I hate being forgotten. If I'm being honest, I had no plans to fall back on, but I can't help but believe I'd fail them anyway… Do I regret making this decision?"

My pen stopped, hovering closely to the pages. I knew I'd hate going about my own life knowing Jake would still have to fight for his life.

My cursive got progressively sloppier as I continued writing.

"Final answer, no. But does my heart agree? Why do I feel so guilty? I made this choice on impulse because it was the right choice. It is the right choice. That day I felt it not only in my heart but in my gut. I have to trust that initial urge... But if I am in the right, then why is my temper short fused, and why can't I be grateful? Why is it that this expectation put on me from others affects me so? Who do I want to please? Who am I failing?"

I waited patiently for a still calm answer... but all I heard was dry-heaving in the bathroom.

I met up with Jake in the living room shortly after. I didn't ask him how he was because quite frankly, that was a stupid question. Instead I asked, "Friends?"

Phase one, Jacob was entertained by "The Office". Phase two, our entertainment was 10 seasons of "Friends" loaned to us by Afton. Though Jacob did not laugh out loud, during the first couple of seasons, he mentioned weeks before that it was a swell distraction. We were already on season nine.

Jacob grunted a "yes."

Somewhat feeling like I was watching alone, I'd often sneak a glance over to him if I thought for sure this scene would make him laugh… yet there was nothing. No extra burst at that.

I noticed it was coffee o'clock, so I walked the imaginary line dividing the living room and kitchen. Getting the contents together, I heard something I was so desperate to hear.

It was a laugh. Small, short, but it was the most beautiful sound I had heard in weeks.

I closed my eyes and smiled, soaking in its wonder and whispered to God, "Thank you."

Game night was fast approaching. Jake wasn't well enough to make the two-hour hall to Austin as his "brothers in pads" were now in the first round of playoffs.

"I am going to go." Friday morning arrived, and Jake was not ready to give in, just yet.

"Buddy, you can't even sit up. How do you expect to watch an entire football game?"

"I am going to go."

"Look, I'll stay with you, and we can listen to it on the radio. I'll even act out the game for you, real time as Lee Graham describes each play. It. Will. Be. Epic."

Jake wasn't taking any of my sarcasm.

"Jess, you'll go, because I am going."

Following his drink of confidence, vomit acted its chaser. He tried holding it in but was unsuccessful.

Not wanting to crush his spirits any further, I told myself, "there's no way he is going."

Jake slept the rest of the day, getting up only once to use the restroom.

Late afternoon, the house filled with cheerful noise, as immediate and extended family made it down that day, as it was also Thanksgiving weekend. Despite efforts, everyone tried respecting Jake's condition and made little mention of him missing out on the excitement. Aunt Lizzie asked if she could stay with Jacob. She, Uncle Denis and our cousins, McKenzie and Maddie, drove in from Midland to take part in our huge family's Thanksgiving traditions. We always looked forward to visits from the Canos.

Lizzie and Denis are the aunt and uncle that would quote "Nacho Libre" and "Napoleon Dynamite" with us. Lizzie was the youngest of Mom's sisters and is well known for her contagious laugh. We knew Jake would be more than happy to wake up to find Lizzie there waiting to hang out with him… but just minutes before we all headed out the door, Jake walked slowly into the living room from his bedroom, using the wall as support. He was dressed in his Fat Boy T shirt, and a coat, buttoned half way, shoes untied but on, Jake mumbled, "I am going to go too." He smiled at all the new faces.

The weakest smile I'd ever seen.

Before taking another step forward, he turned swiftly towards the bathroom and threw up everything he had in his stomach.

He was not going.

His voice, just slightly loud enough to hear behind closed doors said, "I can't make it."

Lizzie nearly cried while uttering, "Jake, is it alright if I stay with you? I am tired from our drive in and would much rather chill here."

"Okay." Jake stayed in the bathroom.

Feeling horrible about leaving him, but also anxious to see the game, and meeting up with the rest of the siblings, we loaded up and headed for Austin.

Uncle Denis and the girls (McKenzie and Maddie, barely two years apart, and not even in middle school) rode with Dad, Mom, Garrett and me. We had much to catch up with our fun company.

One slow hour ticked by with little said between Lizzie and Jake. Aunt Lizzie was always sympathetic and sensitive to what was going on around her. Finally, Jake broke the silence, "Aunt Lizzie?"

"Yes?"

"Can we try again?"

Knowing exactly what he meant, she stood up immediately. "I got the keys right here!" Dangling them as she spoke.

"Is it too late?"

"We'll probably make halftime. That's my favorite part." She smiled. Always knowing what to say.

Jake tied his shoes which he had not removed, then took several deep breaths and closed his eyes waiting for the nausea to pass.

He stood up.

Aunt Lizzie followed close behind him as they made it through the kitchen, laundry room, back room and out the door. Jake hesitated before descending the 6 steps down to the ground. He threw up over the edge of the wooden staircase.

Lizzie did not doubt his motivation and waited patiently as he was doubled over. "It's okay. We've got time."

They stood there a few minutes. Lizzie did not leave his side as she was ready to be his support down the steps. "One at a time." They descended, making it into the vehicle without another incident.

Just before entering the stadium, Denis's phone rang. With his answer "hello" he expressed, "Awesome! We'll see y'all here in a little bit. Drive safe, Liz."

Dad asked, knowing enough from the short conversation. "They're on their way then?"

"They're on their way!" Denis repeated with enthusiasm.

Back in Lizzie's vehicle, Jake had to practice patience now. Though Lizzie was quick witted, her driving was that of an 80-year-old woman rapidly losing eye sight.

Within minutes of the halftime show, Jake and Lizzie walked in, Jake's mask on, careful not to touch anything they sat away from the crowd.

"I feel awesome right now. Thank you, Aunt Lizzie."

Quickly our family found the two troopers and filled the empty spaces around them. Jake's smile was visible through his mask. He jumped up, shouted shouts of encouragement, clapped with excitement and cheered his team to their victory, never becoming faint, dizzy or nauseated.

"That was the most exciting game I have ever seen!" Jake walked without aid back to the vehicle. We all agreed as we found our cars and caravanned back to Mason.

This new strength and happy heart carried on into the wonderful Thanksgiving weekend. No one needed an explanation from where that came...

The family football game, dubbed "Hoerster Turkey Day Classic" consisted of careful planning, draft picking and yearly practice and preparation. We met out on the band practice field. The mothers lined up the lawn chairs, Opa sat in the car due to his allergies getting the best of him and would use the horn as his way of communicating.

Every able-bodied man and women met on the field, flags strapped on, and the strategy would begin.

Jacob volunteered to be the videographer, making the climb up the 12-step platform used by the band instructor. He had the official whistle and officiated from the sky as well as capture every single play by play.

This year, everyone played with their best sportsmanship. NO arguments broke out, and no broken bones. Of course, there was a winner and a loser, but everyone celebrated a common victory,

Jake was feeling awesome.

We watched our game over chili dinner, of which Jake had two helpings.

That evening, Jake and Dad went hunting.

Jacob didn't want to sit and wait, so they hiked, "quite a distance" as my Dad put it. They spotted a deer and tracked it. Jacob shot and killed for meat, he gutted it all on his own.
When Jacob and Dad returned, needless to say, Jacob was a bit tired... but not a fatigued type of tired; it was a normal type of tired, like you and I feel after a day's worth of work.

CHAPTER 18

The Puncher's came up against Goldthwaite again in the second round of play-offs. A hard fought, four quarter, minute-by-minute game, ended in a one-point loss. Though the boys left it all on the field, hope was not lost. We would see them next year.

We welcomed the month of December because that meant Phase Two had finally come to an end. Since Jake opted to enter a study wherein higher dosages of proven medications are administered, this next phase, Phase 3, Interim Maintenance, required stays in the hospital for four days every two weeks. The doctors monitored the positive effects of the treatment against toxicity levels.

Jake was given another opportunity to opt out of the study and continue a standard course, an easier course. Jake's response every time was this, "I've benefited from the courageous battles others have fought and will do the same for others."

Phase 3 was put on hold when Jake's hemoglobin and platelet counts resulted in: "too low to continue." Doctor's ordered two more units of blood and finally sent him home after six hours, without the regular dosage of chemo.

In the spirit of the "giving season" so many people asked how they could help.

Meals continued to come even four months later. Checks for medical bills continued to pour in. Opa single-handedly funded my career as "care-giver," cutting me a check every week.

Each month, it seemed, the insurance company would drop coverage of the drugs Jacob needed. Before we had time to ask, money was donated to help cover medical expenses.

Mom and Dad both worked diligently every day while still finding time to attend Garrett and Elliot's extra-curricular activities, offer Jake support and continue to help out their other children miles away. Each day, Jake would try to do some physical activity. He'd remind me that his muscles missed him and that he'd need to pay them a visit. But, of course, push-ups and burpees were too strenuous for his aching joints and low energy levels. We'd try riding bikes, or walking, sometimes Jake would lift his school books as his weighted bicep curls or over-head press.

A few men on the Mason's Puncher and Cowgirl committee felt Jake would benefit from a bow flex machine, since he had no way of adding resistance training back into his daily routine without compromising his immune system. With half the town rooting for his big return on the football field his senior year, it was hard not to get ahead of ourselves and wish him back to normal, pushing him even though his oncologists were not agreeable to him playing football ever again.

As it was, people poured out their support, eager to give and help out, but just a few days after they loaded the bulky bow flex into our home, the town started buzzing that we were using their money to buy fancy equipment for the entire family to use. It was difficult not to become hurt by these rumors, and still remain grateful to the town's generosity. That same evening as Dad was telling us about the rumor he had heard at work, I voiced to no one in particular, "Well, what will they say next? Especially when we gas up once a week for his visits to the hospital? That we are using it to visit Sea World?"

Mom stayed quiet, and Dad contemplated writing a letter to the newspaper helping to explain our position... yet Jake had a different take on it, softly saying, "What does it matter if we know what's true?" He never looked up from his homework.

Upon the morning's dawn, he would try to work out before commencing his homework, having to decrease the weight ten pounds at a time until finally being able to complete a set. He did not want attention, or to be seen. He just wanted to try.

Rumors did not change his desire to grow stronger.

CHAPTER 19

Grateful for the break in treatment, and with the approaching Christmas season, I couldn't help wanting to "Deck the Halls" with our mixed matched Christmas décor collected from many years past. I left the boys in charge of the lights but as they managed to break more than they could fix, I quickly turned into a control freak and decided to do it all by myself. Jacob laughed, "You are like an ironic Grinch, Jess. You want Christmas, but only your way."

"… and God bless us, everyone." Elliot's jokes weren't always timed well, but this time, he had his brothers laughing along with him. Be it the perfectly timed movie quote, we all decided that once Dad got home from work, "A Christmas Carol" with George Scott would be the movie of choice.

With the holiday fast approaching, even more awareness of the flu season kept Jacob further detached from all of us. He wore his mask indoors, none of us used his bathroom, we wiped the fridge handle after touching it, and visits from friends and family ceased for a while. Though we had our flu shots and washed our hands until they cracked, we couldn't seem to keep all the infections away. Jake and I came down with upper respiratory infections; therefore, I upped the intake of over the counter medications, as Jake's regular regimen was placed on a brief hold.

In this next phase, Phase 3: Interim Maintenance he was to receive a large increase in chemotherapy, along with a lot of IV fluids, so it was imperative that his counts were exactly perfect. So, this phase was postponed... which also meant his full recovery was again, postponed.

Not looking forward to spending four nights at the hospital every two weeks for the next 60 days, Dad and Mom put a lot of effort in making our Christmas traditions last. The presents slowly piled up under the tree, and eggnog became the choice beverage of the house. We anticipated our favorite traditions once our siblings winter break finally commenced. Each room was now packed to its max capacity, as Emilie, Jeb and Hillary chose to stay in Mason for the holiday. As usual, Mom bought the huge can of cheddar, caramel and butter popcorn, and we all found a place to lay or sit comfortably as we started our favorite movie, "It's A Wonderful Life." This movie has been watched every December 24th ever since Emilie was born. We still owned it on VHS. Though there was enough space for us to lie individually, we still sat within inches of one another holding our individual bowls of popcorn.

The next morning, like every Christmas morning, we heard Mom in the kitchen, awaking before all her children to make our favorite breakfast, sausage balls. She'd make over 50, and we'd finish off every last one. We listened to Dad read Luke chapter 1, and for fun, read the final chapter of Jotham's Journey though we had shelved that book years ago when we all "grew up". Slowly, the pile of gifts started to dwindle. Jake was especially anxious to see Garrett open his. We had entered our names into a drawing at Thanksgiving calling it our sibling-gift-exchange. Jake had begged me weeks before to take him to a particular store in Mason though he was not really allowed out in public. We went during a time when the town was not so busy, so Jake could purchase a very particular knife. Jacob had his own money saved from the many times Opa opened his wallet in the giving spirit which seemed his way around us. It would be five dollars here, ten dollars another day, and after many weeks of his generosity, Jake saved quite a bit of money.

As I waited in the car, giving him the space he'd requested, I realized that slowly, almost lost by the inconspicuousness of it, his independence was making a comeback. Not only did it have a positive impact on his overall attitude, but mine as well. Just one month before, I had to assist him while he ate, bathed, and tried to do homework lying down with his eyes closed. I was overjoyed to wait in the car and be on the sidelines, once again, helpless in this situation because this meant that my brother WAS getting better.

Though we had less money to spend, the first Christmas after Jacob's diagnosis felt like we had more than any year, in comparison. It was said at Thanksgiving that we were so grateful Jacob was at the table with us, eating turkey and green bean casserole. It was said again, that we were grateful for the space Jacob took up on the couch, all the popcorn he ate and hearing his voice as we sang Christmas carols. There can never be too little to be grateful for, but we really were blessed with much. Dad shared the final thought that wrapped up the gift-giving for that morning, "It is easy to overlook small things and get caught in the hurried way of life but showing love and being grateful should never be overlooked."

Chapter 20

The end seemed just as far away as when it began. Mom consistently studied Jacob's recovery "road map" so she could plan ahead the days she could take off and the days she couldn't. Jacob preferred knowing as little of the map as possible. He requested we just tell him what each day beheld the night before, so he could focus on school work. Remaining diligent was no ordinary task. It was difficult for him to do this alone without the accountability of his teachers and peers. I did what I could and helped him where I could, but I was no school teacher. Jake's and my differences would come to head and most of our arguments derived from the difference in which we learned.

One extremely rough morning, the day before he and Mom would be leaving for San Antonio, a certain math assignment had both of us stumped. Our voices rose in frustrations, one above the other. This went on, I am sad to admit, for well over 15 minutes. Jake finally held out his hand to say "stop" without words. He took a sip of water, and I did the same. The house was quiet now.

"I have taken my teachers for granted; their jobs are way too important to overlook." Jake's glass had barely left the edge of his lips when he said this. Homeschooling was not my strong suit, and neither was it his.

"I agree, Brother, and I think it is high time you had a proper tutor."

Algebra was a weak subject for me, and thanks to Sherry Keller's ability to teach, I learned enough to graduate. I just wish Jake and I shared her knowledge and love for the subject. Algebra would take up most the day, so the other subjects suffered neglect.

Jake's English teacher was not one to coddle a child just because he was fighting cancer. Be it a way to practice equality among her students, I know not, but I couldn't help feeling it was a bit harsh to say what she did in an email directed at Jake with an attached "F" for failure to complete. She implied that he may have to figure out alternative ways to get the credit, because she doubted he could keep up with her class.

"Let me see that." I grabbed Jake's lap top before he could protest. I read the words silently before Jake could finish reading them out loud. "How heartless!" I exclaimed feeling very defensive for Jacob, "I cannot believe she'd be so heartless!" I felt hot and the only way to cool off was to pace back and forth in my living room or march up to the school and give her a piece of my twenty-year old mind.

Jake asked me to stay put, "Jess, it's okay."

"I can't believe she said you have a poor work ethic. She doesn't see you slave over all this stupid, meaningless work all day while you feel like # ? * ! ! She doesn't know that just a month ago, you couldn't even open your mouth to feed yourself, but somehow you managed to complete her ridiculous assignments!"

"Jess…" Jake tried to reason with me, gently.

"No. No, this is not cool." I ignored his calm manner, "How about I go remind her what Atticus has to explain to his son in To Kill a Mockingbird. She should get that reference, right? I mean, come on, To Kill a Mockingbird is after all an icon for English majors!" I couldn't feel my fingers or toes, and my voice matched that of an intercom. All I could do was shout, "no one can fully understand another person until you walk in his shoes!"

"Jess, stop. I'm not giving you my shoes." He shook me off as I was untying his tennis shoes. "Besides, that's a metaphor."

By this time, Mom returned from work and asked what was going on. I didn't hesitate to tell her every last detail. Just before Mom picked up the phone to "talk it over" Jacob was finally able to speak up. "Mom, please tell her I can do it… I just need a little more time."

It was as simple as that. He didn't feel wronged. My 17-year-old brother understood this situation better than I did. I let my anger get in the way of what was really happening. Mom and I looked at one another and then at the phone. I had to stifle back a laugh as Mom returned the cordless phone to its cradle, with every muscle in her body protesting all the while calmly saying in the most agreeable tone, "I'll sleep on it."

Situations such as that, made it easy for me to see the man Jacob was. He knew he had a duty as a student to finish what was before him. He was determined to graduate with his classmates and was not going to let a little challenge prevent him from doing so.

After agreeing to extend his deadline, just this once, Jake and I also told Mom that he needed real-solid help with algebra. Humbling herself, as asking for help is not easy, Mom made a different phone call. She asked coach Sherry Keller (Hillary's and my track coach) for any online ideas or suggestions. Being a problem solver and caring more for Jake's progression in school than recognition, she suggested something we couldn't believe we hadn't thought of before.

Coach Kahan, a man who substitute taught at the high school and middle school was known by our small town as the most supportive and kind man with a genius brain. He not only attended each football and basketball game, in Mason, but remembered each student's name after only substituting for a class once. He was also seen every day running his favorite route in his favorite town, wearing his Mason Puncher t-shirt, gym shorts and white tube socks. Coach Kahan did not hesitate when asked to start tutoring Jake. He rarely drove, as our home became a regular route for his tennis shoes until the school year ended. This act of kindness allowed Jake to catch up within two weeks and get right back on track. Not to mention, his understanding and appreciation for math increased greatly.

In preparation for his extended stays at the "Hospital Bed Bath and Beyond" as Jake called it, he increased his exercise time from ten minutes to twenty! He knew he was not allowed to really get out of bed as he would be receiving 24 hours of continuous chemotherapy via IV, so he wanted to strengthen his heart every chance he got. Mom arranged to stay with Jake the first night, then I would drive up and remain there until he was discharged. Unsure of what to expect, I was on high alert to make sure I didn't misunderstand instructions given to us by the nurses, or worse, miss any signs that Jake may have organ failure. As the nurse brought in his first bag of chemo, as large as sack of cat food, I couldn't help feeling sick to my stomach. I watched as the yellow stained liquid dripped slowly into my brother's veins. Within an hour, Jake's skin would become pale and scaly. Each bag would drip for 12 hours until empty.

The following morning, I arose from my unsettled sleep from on top the large hard chair and noticed Jake was not in his bed. Before I could panic, he came out of the bathroom and acknowledged me with a, "Good morning, Jess" and continued with a grin, "look the chemo is gone!"

Before I could say, "that is awesome", he grinned again and said proudly, "I am a good chemo sucker."

As the clean, clear liquid made its way down the thin line of tubes leading into his veins, Jake diligently worked on his homework. His nurses would remark, "wow, you are such a good kid, Jacob"

Later that evening, we were relieved to get the final word from the doctor, "Jake is right on track to be cleared for release on Saturday. This particular treatment, 24 hours infused chemo, flushed by 72-hours of fluids has proven more positive results than the standard protocol of treatment. We are going to increase the fluids to lessen the acidity of his urine. This will be confirmation that his body is indeed ridding itself of the chemo."

Jacob looked forward to attending the Hofman's annual Super-Bowl party that Sunday. Having something to look forward to while at the hospital made the long drawn out process go by much faster. No talk of blood or pH counts were discussed. No one told him what he could or couldn't eat. We didn't mention the concern we had for his kidneys and liver undergoing so much trauma from so much chemo. What we focused on was that he felt well enough to completely participate in the party, hang out with some of his buddies, and enjoy some pro football.

Each time we returned to the "Hospital Day Inn", Jake would announce his presence to his adoring audience, telling the ladies at the front desk, "Now, now, I understand you missed me, but I am here now, so no more tears ladies, please." Immediately following, giggles and applause encouraged his light-hearted attitude.

By the evening, the chemo started taking its toll on Jacob. He grew less witty and silly and became quite lethargic. I remained quiet, trying to keep busy and not worry over Jacob too much. I knew by now he did not like that type of attention. The quiet was interrupted with the announcement that Jake would be getting a roommate. A boy, about his age, was diagnosed with leukemia, thirteen days earlier. It would be his first night out of the ICU. His treatment was a bit different as he opted out of the study.

Both Adam and his father, Alex were quiet and respectful but had a lot of questions knowing that this was now our sixth month into treatment. The boys were given strict instructions to use different urinals and sinks. Both their immune systems were compromised, but they didn't want their pee samples to get mixed up. No matter how late at night it was, or random their potty- breaks, they were sure to remind each other whose cups were whose.

Our hospital stays started to fly by as both Jake and Mom and I became hooked on the TV show, "Lost." If we weren't glued to the TV, Jake was doing homework or sleeping. The days we got to be home, he suffered the side effects of the chemo. Sores formed in his mouth and throat and he would get stabbing pains in his back and sides.

Despite the discomfort he would make himself spend at least twenty minutes straining his muscles on the bow flex machine, though the amount of weight was nowhere close to how strong he wanted to be. We'd go on bike rides. Jake would push to go further and further. His breathing became heavy, his body wanted to quit, but he would not turn back until he went as far as his goal.

CHAPTER 21

Seven months into remission marked the end of Phase Three. Dad read to us that morning while we ate our breakfast, "Better is the end of a thing than its beginning, and the patient in spirit is better than the proud in spirit." Ecclesiastes 7:8. Eager for phase four, Delayed Intensification, to begin, Dad explained almost verbatim how Dr. Geo described this phase, "its design is to treat any remaining resistant leukemia cells by regular chemo treatments through lumbar puncture at least once a week. It will still require daily oral medication and intra-muscular injection as well as increased dosages of steroids."

"Ugh, more steroids." I thought. Out of the poisonous chemotherapy and the organ supporting steroids, Dexamethasone and Prednisone were Jake's least favorite. On the kitchen counter, the new pill bottles took up most of the "dead space" near the large calendar and cordless phone, and that basket meant for pens and pencils, but seemed to collect everything but intended. The labels read "Sulfameth, Trimethoprim, Clonazepam and Dexamethasone. Though I could now read the labels without stuttering over myself, I learned quickly the side-effects my brother would suffer. Medications were the necessary evil.

"The final ten days of this phase, he will receive cranial radiation." Dad cleared his throat and began eating once again. Jake offered his thoughts immediately, "great, now I am going to be bald and fat."

The boys thought this was funny and tried holding back their cereal and milk from leaving their mouths.

Mom, Jake and Dad would leave later that morning to discuss the number of visits to San Antonio required, and the expectations the doctors had of him, plus the expectations we had for Jake's journey back to "normal". The subject of football had not been brought up much at home, yet, it always remained a possibility in Jake's heart. Dad played football in high school, and absolutely loved getting to see all his boys play. He'd say it is just one of the many highlights of being a father to boys. Dad and Jake couldn't help but ask once the doctor finished his spiel, after all the doctor did just say Jake was responding so well to the treatment.

"The season starts in just over four months…" Dad explained. "I mean, we know it would be so difficult for him, and we don't expect as much out of him, but would it be possible for him to suit up?"

A long pause from the doctor discouraged Jake. Until then, Jake did not realize how badly he wanted to play again until he saw in Dr. Geo's face that football was out of the picture.

"The porta-cath in his chest is too high a risk alone for such a physical sport. If we stick to this regimen of treatment however, by basketball season, we will have already removed the port, and he will have enough time to heal by his first district game." The doctor, probably feeling like he was giving good news, patted Jake's back,

"I can't wait to hear the stories about you getting your dunk back on."

The ride back home was quiet. All Dad could say was, "I am sorry, Buddy. We love you."

Little was said about football, especially in the Bibb household. Elliot and Garrett tried not to project their excitement for the upcoming season too much onto Jake's disappointed spirit. Instead, Jake spent a lot of time on a new hobby relating to one of his favorite shows, "Man vs Wild." Jake had always loved the outdoors, but with the frequent visits to Bass Pro Shop, and spending money given to him by Opa, and birthday savings, Jake stocked up on camping and hunting supplies. The first week of phase four was one of the worst for Jake. The steroids and several injections of chemo took a toll on his body and mood.

About to lose it with the stomping around, huffing and puffing and slamming doors I finally asked kindly, "Where's the grinning Jacob who says please and thank you?"

Answering in third person, "He is gone, and this one has a raw butt from having diarrhea all night and all day the past week but still manages to be fat somehow!"

"I can buy you some soothing wipes."

"Okay, but how does that help my puffiness?"

"Jake, that will go away soon. Need I remind you that you are on seven different oral medications all with temporary side effects?"

"No, you need not." Enunciating every word from annoyance.

"Well, I miss the other Jacob."

"I do too."

That was the only time Jacob ever wished aloud for something different than the cards handed to him.

"Hey, tomorrow marks the last day you have to take steroids."

No response. Instead, Jake returned to the sharpening of his knives.

The next morning, Jacob woke up before I did from excruciating pain. Mom was heating up rice socks in the microwave as Jacob's eyes squinted in response to the shooting pains in his knees and ankles.

"Bad morning?" I questioned the obvious. Jacob did not respond but Mom looked flustered.

"Jacob has joint pains."

Not surprised by this as this was the most common complaint, I was confused as to why she was seemingly more worried, I had nothing better planned than to offer my services. I walked over to Jacob to ask if he needed anything. As I approached nearer him, it was hard to miss the swelling in his knees and ankles. I guess my face told Jake it really did look bad as he responded to my reaction, "it feels like an evil person got hold of a sledge hammer and keeps on banging it against my knee."

I propped up his legs with every pillow I could find. Mom and I took turns getting him anything he requested from more lemonade, to pickles, to turning on the Cosby show, more lemonade, corn dogs, heat up the rice sock, then cooling it off… up, down and up, down. Every single time, Jake would say, "Thank you."

Several days passed, and the joint pain and swelling finally subsided. On mornings when he felt well, I'd stay in my room a little longer to give the boys some space. I made note that they really had not had much time throughout this entire journey to spend time just with each other. They missed their brother driving them to school, seeing him in the halls, and seeing him play. Rather than hearing "wishes" I heard laughter, deep belly laughter. To this day, I will not ask what was so funny. There are some moments meant to be shared only with brothers.

Most weeks, Jacob did his homework diligently and without being reminded. Others, though, it was like pinning down an unruly two-year-old to change his diaper.

"It is Saturday, so I don't have to."

"You do because last week's suffering put us behind schedule."

"No, it didn't." Jake retaliated confidently while sharpening the machete.

"Seriously, Jake? In my book, if you have energy to sharpen your knives, you have enough energy to do your homework."

"It is different. I like sharpening my knives, but I don't like doing my homework."

"You sound like a teenager."

"I am one. But unlike most teenagers, I have hemorrhoids."

Trying not to laugh out loud, I voiced, "All I want is for you to finish your home-work, so we can do something fun together."

"And all I want," now breaking into a song, "is a room somewhere, far away from the cold night air…"

Waiting him for him to finish his "My Fair Lady" solo I interjected, "you would have been finished by now."

"Jess, it's like 10:00AM. I have all day to finish it as I am homeschooled and do not work."

By this time, I had some housework to do, so I grabbed the vacuum from the back room, and started to clean up.

"JESS!" Jacob screamed over the noise of the vacuum. Reluctantly turning it off, "What?" I felt annoyed and felt I should show it.

"When I become bald, are you going to shave your head too, to support me?" Jacob acted earnest.

"Absolutely not." Finding the power switch, and just before clicking it back on, he spoke again, "I think I have fever." Now, he had my full attention.

"Jake, are you serious?" I walked towards him to feel his forehead.

"Cabin fever." He smirked.

"Ugh, do not do that." I rolled my eyes. "why don't you do your homework outside."

"It's raining."

That was the first time I had noticed.

"When I get to go back to school, I am not going to come inside this house but to sleep. But maybe not even then. I might just sleep on the trampoline."

"Or you could go camping for a week when your doctors release you, and then you can just live normally." I tried to get back to vacuuming, again.

"Oh, I will go camping! That's a great idea! But first, I better finish my homework, please quit distracting me." Jake's spirits seem to lift as he tossed another smirk my way. I playfully acted annoyed, when deep down I was so happy to see that the swelling in his ankles and knees was minimal and his mood was brighter.

Hillary visited home as many times as she possibly could and would jump into whatever routine we had going on. She was excited to attend one of Jacob's appointments that morning. On the ride over, Mom and I sat back and enjoyed listening to Hillary and Jake share stories. It was obvious Jake was feeling much better compared to the beginning of this phase. He had also seemed to be losing the puffiness that had him distraught a few weeks back.

"Well, after this phase, is the maintenance phase and then I get to go back to school!" Jacob's voice squeaked just a little with excitement.

"What about Prom. Do you get to go?"

"Yea, I already have a hot date."

"Oh, really, who is it? Dyllan?" Hillary threw back some sarcasm.

"Actually, yea. We've been planning for months." We all giggled as we knew Jacob missed his friends more and more every day.

"It depends on his counts, but the doctor did say it was a possibility." Mom tried to keep realities in check as kindly as she could.

"Hey, how many months have I been doing this?" Jake grew silent as if to count the months and answer himself, but Hillary responded fairly quickly,

"Seven or eight. Why?" She knew Jake was curious how many months it had been since his diagnosis as reflecting back wasn't quite his main priority.

"It's like almost as long as a Fraternity Leave."

Hillary and I laughed immediately at the play on words, unsure why we thought it was so funny.

Mom said, behind her laughter that there is actually something called "Paternity Leave" and that it is shorter than Maternity Leave. Jacob laughed at his mix up,

"Okay, yea, that's what I meant then… So, did Dad get Paternity Leave seven times?" (Jake dramatically enunciated the "p" in paternity).

"No, or else we would have had to take leave from our house." Mom's wit was always timed well.

Hillary finally got to meet Dr. Geo. She was the final sibling to have the honors. Dr. Geo impressed her with his memory, "Let's see, there is the oldest sister, Emilie, in Boerne, the big brother, Jeb who also graduated from A&M, she," pointing at me, "Jess or Hey Again" I winked as he continued, "Elliot is the quarterback, and Garrett is the little one that likes Wii sports." He patted Jacob on the back, "and this is guy will officially be starting radiation next week." This wasn't exactly the news we wanted to hear, but it did mean that phase four was almost over.

Losing hair is a well-known result of radiation. We were all so prepared for it to fall out in the beginning, but when it did not, we felt it safe to assume his hair would hang on until the end. So, Dad, Bibb brothers, friends and the Fat Boys, were on stand-by. Jake tipped the scale at 228 pounds after his third visit with the radiology oncologist. At the beginning of the phase, he was 245 pounds. His worries of being bald and fat had diminished with his water weight.

Jacob and I decided to stay at Emilie's for the duration of this process as driving back and forth from Mason four days in a row just was not frugal. As Em and I were preparing dinner, Jacob had a lot of energy that evening so he started pacing around trying to figure out what to do. Casually, Jacob wiped his hand over his head, and out came a huge chunk of 1.5-inch-long golden hair. We all stared at it for a while without saying or doing anything.

Like a lighting flash, Jacob darted outside and continued to run his hands through his hair. Chunks and more chunks floated to the ground. I fed off of his positive enjoyment. He kept saying things like, "This is so cool!" and "Wow, it feels so breezy."

Bit by bit I saw less of his blonde/golden hair and more of his white head. He was not sad or shocked… he just kept pulling it off like lint from a shirt. To the beat of one of his favorite songs, he put a twist on it and sang, "I'm too sexy for my hair, too sexy for my hair I just don't care" He shook his backside with the rhythm.

We were outside for over an hour mesmerized by how much hair would fall to the ground. He pulled out groups of thirty to forty blonde hairs. We played "odd or even" with one chunk and we counted 31. Jacob guessed correctly.

I watched long enough that I felt comfortable to have a try at it. As if I was combing his hair to one side, my fingers held many long strands of hair. Just like that. Emilie joined us with the clippers she used at school to shear animals. We made a video to upload onto Facebook per Jacob's request. While I was shaving his head, it hit me that my little brother was about to be bald. Each row I went over with the clippers, the easier his hair came off. The clippers really didn't even have to work. Once his head shone with the last ray of the sun, Emilie and I were inevitably shocked. Not that he was bald, but that he looked really good! He was also amazed at the transformation and admired it just a little... one could say.

He put on his sunglasses and held his machete and posed for another picture. (I have never seen him this camera happy) Then he asks rhetorically, "what now, Van Diesel? You ain't got nothing on me."

Among all the excitement Jacob called up his best bud and said, "dude, it happened."

Dyllan's initial reaction was denial, but then spread the word to everyone else, one week before prom, they all would be bald.

After Jake made the phone call home, Dad grabbed his clippers immediately. Elliot had the hardest time with the idea of shaving his own head. He asked Jacob to keep as much hair as possible for as long as possible, but Jake said, "too late, the patches were hideous!"

Final call was to Jeb. Overjoyed to participate, the pictures started to flood the internet. One of our favorites was in Julie Gillespie's kitchen. Several large football players, including her son Luke, who is Garrett's age, had sought her skill in shaving heads. She had commented that "she'd prefer to have not seen that much of her child's scalp as some of these boys just did not look good without hair." Jake felt more and more supported by these guys willing to sacrifice their good looks just to say, "you're not alone."

We had two more weeks of his four consecutive days of clinic visits consisting of the Aca-C process. Mom used to do this one at home, but since there was a shortage, the FDA had restrictions on the dosage so only healthcare professionals could administer the drug. Though Jake was weaker, he felt less and less pain in his joints, so he worked out as often as his body would let him.

Mom drove Jake to his visit which marked the end of phase four. Jake was anxious to feel normal again and had two requests on his mind. He so badly wanted to attend his Junior Prom and go to school again. The doctors based every decision around his blood counts.

Dr. Geo entered the room with good news. "Jake, you're going to need to rent a tux, you are going to prom!"

"For real?!" Jake and Mom asked this at the same time.

"Yes, and not just that, you have responded so well, that it looks like you'll be finishing your spring semester with the rest of your peers." Dr. Geo said this with a giant smile across his face.

The next week, Mom drove Jacob to Brady, the nearest town with a Department of Motor Vehicles office, to renew his license, and the next morning, with the boys buckled in the back seats, Jake drove his brothers to school for the first time since September 3rd, 2010.

Just like that, Jacob no longer needed a full-time caregiver. As arrangements were being made for me to move in with Emilie, and start school again in the fall, I couldn't help but be so glad for Jake's recovery. Though he had many a disappointment, and quite the up-hill battle, his days of crippling nausea were over. Now his challenge was rejoining the normalcy of a high school teenager, while remembering to take his medications for the next two years. Plus, living with minor aches and pains.

CHAPTER 22

As the school year wrapped up, Emilie and I enjoyed the weekly visits from Mom and Jacob and sometimes Dad as it was still necessary for Jake to receive chemo through his port, until one evening over dinner, we were surprised to hear that Jake would be going into surgery at the end of June to have his port removed.

"What? Why? I thought he still needed treatment." Concerned and feeling totally out of the loop now, I questioned the seemingly good news.

Instead of Mom or Dad responding, Jake answered with a mouth full of spaghetti. "Well, it so happens that the doctors will not let me play football with the porta-catheter in, so they will need to take it out."

"Football?" Emilie re-iterated, just as confused as I was.

"In July they will run some tests. He will have been in Maintenance phase for at least three months. The doctors have seen a high percentage of patients regain their health and strength during this phase.

They hope the same for Jacob, so we will know more next month." Mom, again with the reality check.

"Until then, Jake gets a three week break from chemo, so his immune system can build up before going into surgery." Dad offered more good news.

"Yea, and Dad and I are going to start working out, so I can get a head start on my football bod." Jake sucked in his stomach and flexed both his arms for us while saying this.

"This is such great news!" Emilie and I said this at the same time.

I started working as a nanny for one of Jacob's nurses' three nieces, but so much of me missed Jacob and the first-row seat to the excitement of his journey. I made frequent visits to Mason. Father's Day weekend I planned to arrive in Mason the same time Hillary would. Jacob was a little tired from his therapy the day before so was not as chirpy as the last time I saw him. The boys, Dad and Hillary and I decided to go up to the school to shoot some hoops. We figured Jake would sit this one out, but when he caught on to what was going on he jumped up and said, "Wait for me!"

Instead of basketball, we decided to hit the practice field. We had a Frisbee and a football and leisurely threw it back and forth to one another. Jacob picked up the football and started jogging to the opposite end zone, while shouting back to us, "my body forgot how to sprint, so I am going to remind it how to!"

We all watched as he started out slowly, then gradually picked up the pace as he went 10, 20, 30 then 60 yards. His legs looked like noodles, but his arms seemed to have accepted the idea of sprinting really well. Winded and sweaty, he walked/jogged back to us, "what are you bums standing around for?"

Matching Jake's motivation, the boys started calling out routes. Elliot was the quarterback and would tell us where to go or what to do. After several minutes of this, Garrett asked to be the quarterback and enjoyed the honor of giving orders. Jake ran the suggested route, but as the launched throw was just a bit too quick for Jake to catch, we all watched it land opposite side of the sprinkler system strategically placed on the sidelines. The long thin pipes stood maybe three inches above the now brown, splattered with green, bladed lawn where we'd been playing. Jacob made sure we were all watching him when he moved to retrieve the ball. He was maybe five feet from the ball. It would require him to step over the pipe, bend over, pick up the ball and pass it back to Garrett. Instead, Jake got a running start and made a gigantic leap over the tiny pipe to assure a clear landing free from tripping over this imaginary hurdle.

We could not contain our laughter at his dramatic gesture in trying to look agile and athletic. Jacob acted happier and more energetic than we had seen him in a very long time. It was so encouraging seeing him tackling Garrett, jogging around, throwing the football and making great catches from Elliot.

The following morning Jacob gathered us all around for an important message, "Operation Jacob's recovery will consist of lots of milk and protein shakes, lifting and sprints as I need to be back in shape as of yesterday! We may call it, OJR. Everyone will need to participate whether it be lifting weights with me or giving me high fives. I will take whatever I can get. Thank you and meeting adjourned."

Jake's motivation from this point on was just a foreshadowing of what was the mark of a new beginning for him. Dad put it this way, "Every journey we take through life has a beginning and an end. Each moment of the day in each day of each week of every month of every year contain little beginnings and endings. As one journey concludes, a new one begins. Some of the journeys of life are fun and enjoyable. Some are not. Both are necessary, and God's sovereignly reigns over all these moments. To quote Newt Gingrich, 'Perseverance is the hard work you do after you get tired of doing the hard work you already did.'"

Jacob told Dad in the middle of a difficult work out, "Even if I don't get to play, getting to suit up with my teammates is a victory in and of itself."

CHAPTER 23

Deep in my being I took every precaution to not get "caught" again, but as the summer raced by and the 2011-2012 school year commenced, I was back to worrying about bills, my own education and future. I adjusted quickly to the fast pace living as a nanny to a successful and talented family. Each day there was an event, tap or ballet practice, a voice lesson, a photo-shoot, or a commercial audition. I'd pick them up from their beautiful home, drop them off at three different schools, just in time to start picking them up again. With the unlimited credit card given to me at the same time as their house keys and nanny mobile, we'd snack on Chick-fil-a every day, keep the nanny-mobile gassed up, and get groceries plus any other necessities for after school projects. I got paid to taxi them around San Antonio, bring them home safely and help them with home-work, right until their parents came in the door.

Emilie and I spent every evening visiting together and though she had a three-bedroom house, we shared hers. Jeb had adjusted well to his life in Austin and couldn't wait until the day he and

Katherine would wed. Hillary faced a difficult decision over the summer after she injured her back while pole-vaulting, forcing her track career to come to a complete end. Hardin-Simmons in her rear view, she moved back home, taking my place in the bedroom across from Jake's. She was leaving more than an aspired track career behind. Her boyfriend, Todd and she had become "intended" as Opa would say. A long-distance relationship would only prove their relationship strong. Her plan was to work with Mom at the dentist office and save that money, so she could continue her studies at UTSA, and then she and Todd would get married. Hillary loved to plan years ahead. Football was again the conversation around the dinner table with the boys. Jacob gladly adopted back the normal pace of life, yet his dosage of medicine didn't always agree with his breakfast.

As much as I hated to admit it, I felt like I was slowly forgetting what largely affected us in 2010. How could that be? I kept telling myself, I'd never forget what Jake had to go through, or how often God reminded me of His love and mercy. As if I'd gotten caught again, I was rushing around San Antonio, trying to find the right book for one of my girls. I thought for one quick instant that I couldn't believe my life had come to this; finding the newest copy of this 12-year-old's favorite author was the "most important thing"?

Finally, after much help from a lady in a green vest, we found the book and made our way to the blue nanny-mobile. Emilie called me. It was the middle of the day, just after school would have let out for her high-school students. Still too early for her to be home, so I was curious. Had she run out of gas again? Did she want to go see a movie after I got off of work?

"What's up, sis?" I was hoping she'd say, "movie."

"Where are you, right now?" Her voice mimicking one I'd heard just shy of a year prior.

"Oh, no. What's wrong?" I made a mental check-list of every member of my family with Jake's name at the top. Concerned greatly of hearing the word, "relapse".

"Oma was admitted to the hospital with abdominal pains. They believe they have found a tumor on her stomach." Emilie sounded scared yet calm all at the same time.

"Oma?" I was surprised. Never had I ever seen her with even a cold. I wasn't scared. I wasn't angry. I felt nothing like I felt when I first heard the news about Jacob. I didn't know what to feel first. Worried? Confused? Disbelief?

"Where is she?" I knew I didn't want her to be alone.

"She's in Round Rock. Mom and our Aunts and Uncle are already there with Opa. I already found a substitute teacher for tomorrow. I'd like to visit her tonight."

That night we found her resting in her bed, greeting us with a smile as we entered. I felt like all this was too familiar and too soon, yet when I held my Oma's hand, and Em held the other, I saw she had already come to peace with everything. Jacob agreed he recognized this look and explained that when he'd prayed earlier that day, "she, like me, had practice receiving God's will and grace, and though this diagnosis was a shock to us all, it was almost like her heart was already in heaven, ready to meet her maker."

The moments piled up as we waited for the doctors to rule out her prognosis as "terminal".

Mom, in the same position as she was for Jacob, took care of all the details, arranged the appointments with the doctors, and translated the terminology so we'd all know and understand what was going on.

"The CT scan had already shown multiple tumors growing on her stomach lining. Once they take the biopsy we will know if it is treatable."

Since we all couldn't stay in the hospital that night, we did our waiting, all together in Oma and Opa's cabin. Each moment felt like the last, full of questions.

Finally, the phone rang, and Mom answered with her little black notebook for writing down key facts, and reports. We wanted our Oma to stay with us here on earth, we weren't ready to let her go. Oma was so calm, as if one answer would not affect the other. Opa, was not as calm. He wanted to blame himself for her getting sick. Mom hung up the phone and re-iterated what she'd heard. "Good news!" We all cheered before hearing the rest of the facts. "The biopsy further proved that this type of cancer, Gastro-Intestinal Stromal Tumor can be treated with an oral chemo pill called, Gleevec. She'll start it immediately."

How quickly our prayers were answered. As far as we knew, we didn't have to say "good-bye" just yet. Mother continued, "the hope is to avoid surgery until the tumors shrink. Then to remove part of the stomach to further the chances of it not coming back."

We seemed to only alter our lives just a little to help Oma recover. With each member of the family helping out, it made her recovery seem to go by so quickly, mixing in with the excitement of the new season coming up.

At the beginning of August, the doctors removed Jacob's portacath just in time for him to step on the field for two-a-days. Though Jake couldn't keep up with his team's agility, and already well conditioned bodies, he focused on one drill at a time, determined to get faster and stronger each day. Having been a year since he stressed his body so, he not only understood, but could feel the reasons why the doctors put such strict limitations on his football career.

He had to pick either offense or defense, as hydration and rest between series was critical. He absolutely could not play both ways as he had been accustomed to do. The doctors would only allow him to practice and play on Friday nights if his weekly platelet and white blood cell counts were in perfect range.

Despite how he felt, he could not skip a single dose of medication. The doctors also reminded him that his body has already been through so much trauma that adding too much unnecessary strain on it is not recommended. "Start slow and be patient with yourself. You will most likely not gain back all the strength you had before this." The oncologist's words did not convince Jacob.

His first week back, Jacob told us, "It was like my 7th grade year all over again but I think I was stronger then." Each day Jake got up from his slumber to play catch up. His school work had doubled in difficulty and homework assignments, while his body slowly adjusted to the new routine of early mornings, school and football practice twice a day. His muscles were weak. His heartrate had not seen above the ninety's in a long while. His coordination had to be practiced, repeated and continued. His footwork also took more time to catch up with his determined will. When he lifted weights, he struggled past the weakness and fatigue. He'd add more and more weight each week, slowly getting stronger.

His teammates recognized the determination and pushed each other, obtaining their own personal records. It seemed the entire team was relentlessly pushing forward, even early on into the season, these boys were not looking back. Dyllan, the strong tackle for the Mason Punchers, and Jake's best friend, wrote an essay for an assignment describing the Puncher's Heart:

When one reflects upon the people who have made an impact in their lives the average answer is usually a close family member, teacher or famous role model. But rarely, as in my case, do you find your biggest influence to be your best friend. And until my junior year, he never would have been. I love football, the mixture of brutality and strategy has always been more than just appealing to me. And, although not trying to brag, it just so happens that I'm not too shabby at it either. Living in a town as small as mine, football and ranching are just about the only two topics anyone gives a hoot about. "You got to Puncher up not Eagle down!" my father always says. And so, like him and his father before him I have tried my best to carry on that "Puncher football legacy," which includes slobber-knocking hitting and most importantly the will to never quit. Now I had the hitting down to a T, and I thought I had that fighting drive down as well, but as we rolled into my junior year with state bound expectations, I found out what true puncher heart was all about. I was a big boy, fairly strong and athletic, but if you were able to double every attribute I had and combine it into one body Jacob Bibb, one of my best friends, is the man you would create. I always admired

Jacob and the way he played the game, but I never looked into the true commitment he put into it. He started both ways during our second game of the season and every timeout that he was called he would be on the sidelines puking out more than I thought any man could hold. But when coach asked if he needed a break the answer would always be, "no." We won the game and Jacob continued to throw up the whole way home and all of us just figured he had the bug that had been making its rounds around town. That Monday as we were lifting I was feeling a little sore and told my sick partner Jacob that I was going to take a break and skip out on the last few sets. The words he then told me I will never forget. "Come on man! I'm sick and I'm doing it!" Now at the time those words had just flown through one ear and out the other, but three days later they came back and made their everlasting impression in my memory as we found out that Jacobs "little flu" was actually leukemia. That news hit everyone deep. Who knew that this high school junior who was playing his heart out one week earlier had actually been sick with leukemia the whole time? That simple statement he said in the weight room now had a completely new meaning. If a person diagnosed with leukemia could work harder than a fully capable me, then obviously I needed to do a little soul searching of my own. That Friday we played the undefeated and highly ranked Bobcats and the odds were against us. But when I thought about my teammate and friend laying in that hospital bed wanting nothing more than to be on the field with his team, I finally realized what true "Puncher Heart" was all about. Never had I played a game so hard in my life, and when the final buzzer sounded, and the scoreboard showed us ahead by two, I for once could actually say I left it all on the field. Now, a year and a hundred chemo treatments later, Jacob has been able to return to school, regain his strength, and even play some more football. In fact, you could probably say everything has returned to normal. But if you were to ask me, I would have to respectfully disagree. Because of the heart he showed through those tough times and the influence that has had on my life, Jacob Bibb has given me a new understanding of hard work, dedication, and faith which can and will carry me through whatever obstacles that stand in my way. To me, his story alone is all the influence I will ever need. Jacob Bibb is a living example of "Puncher Heart."

In the hearts of the Punchers and our town, the year 2011 will not be forgotten. Not only is it the season known for great victory, but it's the season we all got to witness a second chance. This group of boys had talent and chemistry bound with passion that no other team has shown. Jacob remained on the sidelines the majority of his senior year, cheering his team on to victory after victory. With each mile traveled, or each minute spent on our home turf, the town of Mason supported the Punchers and coaching staff every step of the way.

The first game of the season was at home, against our rival, the Junction Eagles. Each day the boys spent in the scorching heat over the summer and into late August built up to this moment. The moment that would set the tone for the 2011 Puncher football season. The home side stadium was packed full, such is the case, historically. Play-by-play, drive-by-drive, the Punchers pushed the ball in for touchdown after touchdown, extra point by point. Our defense stopped the Eagles one down at a time keeping them far from their end zone. By the fourth quarter, the scoreboard read 38 to 0.

Number 44 kept his helmet on the entire game, standing taller than all his teammates on the sideline, his muscles filling out his jersey once again. Knowing at the beginning of the week he'd get to play, since his blood counts were at the acceptable level, and his coaches were on board with his comeback, yet cautious of over-working or risking any injury. His teammates geared up for the moment Jake would return to the field, just as excited as he.

From the stands, we watched the head coach walk over to #44, put his hand on his helmet, leaning in telling him something, then seconds later, patting his back as Jake hustled to the line of scrimmage.

The entire crowd stood up and cheered, creating a noise so great that it filled your entire being.

Tears streamed down cheeks, and hearts lept at the witnessing of a second chance! Jacob describes that moment as if it was from a movie, "When Coach finally called my name, just seconds before releasing me to the field, he told me with the most genuine look in his eyes, that he was proud to share this moment with me! As soon as my first step planted on the gridiron, it felt like I was walking in a dream with the thunderous roar of the crowd behind me to my teammates greeting me on the field. I couldn't hear myself think."

Tear-filled eyes, and large grins watched anxiously for what would happen next. The boys assumed their positions, defending the line. Elliot, number 12, on the left as outside linebacker and Jacob on the right as defensive end, with the nine other mighty Punchers all with the same goal in mind, "defend and protect". Their eyes watched the second snap of the series, with their bodies following instantly, knowing exactly what to do. The ball stayed in the hands of the Eagle's quarterback, trying strong side where Elliot met him with his pads colliding into his chest, keeping him just shy of a five-yard gain. The third down, the Eagles would try for the opposite side, giving it to their runningback to rush up the middle. Jacob was met with a block, as the runningback made just two steps past the now hole. What looked like a clean break for the Junction Eagles, Jake surprised both teams, and both sides of the stadium when he broke free from the block just enough to reach out and grab the running back's arm and pull him down forcing them into fourth down.

His team rushed towards him, chest bumping, hugging and patting him on the back, while the crowd cheered again, loud enough so you couldn't hear yourself think. This tackle was just one of many that night already performed by talented teenagers, but it was this tackle that each person shared a little bit of their own victories. In one small moment in time, lasting just a few seconds, all the hardship, pain, all the prayers and support from the year prior, entered into this moment making it last longer and longer in our hearts! It reminded us all that Jacob did not fight this battle alone.

Jake soaked up every second, overjoyed to be with his team again. Elliot, so anxiously waiting for this moment, truly believing, even back when Jake couldn't move on his own, that he would get to play again, could barely keep his composure! The referee standing next to Elliot asked, "Who is number 44? Is he famous or something?" Elliot answered the best way he knew how, as he watched Jake jog back towards the sideline, "ha ha, no sir. That's my brother, Jacob Bibb."

Just before reaching the sidelines to stand back with his teammates, Jacob looked up at the crowd, then up to the sky as his fist shot up to the sky; pointing towards the only One that could have made that moment possible. With his heart beating loudly in his chest, feeling more alive, and also winded, he said, "thank you!"

CHAPTER 24

The Punchers marched on, one victory after the next, defeating the teams that had defeated us the season before. One step after the next, no-one was looking back, and now had sights on "Jerry's World" where the State Finals were to be held. Each Friday night, the boys would show more strength, more stamina, and more heart. Before we knew it, we were making arrangements to go to Arlington, Texas. The Punchers had made it to the State Finals for the first time in Mason's football history!

KXAN news station found their way to Mason to follow the story of the long journey our boys had made to the UIL 2011 High School Football State Championship Finals. They filmed people walking on the square, business owners, filmed the Pep-rally and interviewed several of the seniors all for the following evenings broadcast. The reporter found it incredible that our starting center, Brodey Taylor, had one arm. When asked if this was a challenge, we all knew what his answer would be, "I've never felt like I have a disadvantage." Not only is he a powerful player, but extremely coordinated. Often, he'd be seen driving his standard truck around town eating a hamburger at the same time.

As the reporter put it, "The Mason Punchers are used to persevering in tough times." It was too surreal to see our country boys on the regional news station being interviewed by Jacqueline Ingles. With the added interest of the "one-armed center" and the "Linebacker and Cancer survivor" the reporter had enough for a story. Seeing Jacob on television, as calm, cool and collected, as if the large camera was not in front of his face, answered one of her inquiries just like he was speaking to me, "the Lord has just blessed me with returning my strength." He wasn't looking for sympathy, nor was he interested in any more attention, Jake was ready to play ball.

The town of Mason had never been so quiet in the middle of the day. Nearly every business closed their doors Thursday the 15th of December with similar verbiage on varying make-shift signs, "gone to Jerry's World". Over half of the population car pooled, caravanned or took a charter bus all the way to Arlington. I know in my own family, though we car pooled, we had four or five different vehicles, each at maximum capacity.

It appeared to take only a few minutes for over 5000 people to fill in the seats of the Cowboy Stadium. Home-made posters were held up in the sky, shouts were made trying to get loved one's attention, all while the boys were warming up on the field. Though they were teenage boys in peek condition, they looked so small down on the field. I couldn't make up my mind whether to look at the boys on the field or to look up at the jumbotron. One half of the entire stadium seemed to be painted in purple and white while the other, in Stamford Bulldog blue. Once again, family was all together again, plus the added bonus of Dad's side of the family. His Aunt Earlene and Uncle Bussie lived in Dallas for 60 plus years. Aunt Earlene, though older, and weaker, still appeared a mighty woman in our eyes. She had been battling Chronic Lymphocytic Leukemia since 2009, but one would not know this by looking at her or talking to her. She, as sharp as a tack, had a smile that could penetrate the saddest of souls and bring them out of any rut. As if on the front line with the boys herself, she was ready to witness a victory. This victory would not be of a 1A UIL football championship alone, but of one defying the odds, persevering though it hurts, and celebrating second chances.

The Bulldogs held an overall record of 13-3, having the advantage of speed and a strong defensive game. The Punchers carried an undefeated record with the advantage of... well, being Punchers. Their heart for their teammates, their love of the game, and having never looked back, the Punchers did what they knew how to do. Yard by yard, not changing any part of their offense or defensive strategies, they drove the ball to a 62 to 40 win over the Bulldogs.

Not having to muster up any form of gratitude, each football player gleamed with the overwhelming experience of getting to participate in such an event. When asked how it felt to play and win the state championship, we'd hear, "I feel so privileged" or "I am honored to have been a part of this."

Proud to have been a Puncher, Jacob held the trophy high in the sky! Though he no longer was one of the strongest players, nor did he lead the Punchers in sacks, in fact, he hardly played his senior year. It was not about what he couldn't do anymore. No. Instead, it was about from where he had come. He no longer had to wear a mask when attending public places. That trophy, held up with now strong arms, represented Jake no longer having to isolate himself at the football games, cheering from distant places. It was more about him standing on the field, rather than hunched over the toilet. It was the brotherhood, love and support that kept Jake smiling, even during the most difficult of times. It meant God was still writing his story.

More challenges and hurdles would come his way, but that is not what mattered. No matter how many times he was knocked down or put on a different path Jacob always would say, "no matter what happens to me, I want people to know that God is always merciful."

This story, like all stories, can be told from many different perspectives, but if we look hard enough, we'd see that God held the pen the entire time. I, along with many others, wanted to control the outcome of my brother's diagnosis, but God had a better plan.

It wasn't death he was afraid of, nor the long journey to recovery. No. For Jake the fear was forgetting Who was with him, and Who was fighting for him.

God continued to show His Mighty Heart, reminding him with the dawn of each day, "Do not be afraid."

Eight years later, this book, once finally published, will enter Jake's hands as a married man.

Chick-Fil-A donated much during Jake's "Play for Jake" campaign in 2010, yet the blessings did not stop there. Jake started working at Chick-Fil-A while attending Texas State University, at the same time a beautiful girl named, Evelyn Villarreal also started working there; while putting herself through school as a journalist major. Upon introduction, their two worlds collided.

Having almost everything in common, it was just a matter a time before the two should wed. On March 17th 2018, two hearts became one. Congratulations to Mr. and Mrs. Jacob Bibb! We all prayed for your life to be spared, but God didn't stop there. His handy-work knitted together your happily-ever-after.

Friday, Sept. 24th
5pm-8pm

Come eat and give us your receipts! Chick-Fil-A will give us 20% of the profits from the receipts to help Jake fight leukemia!

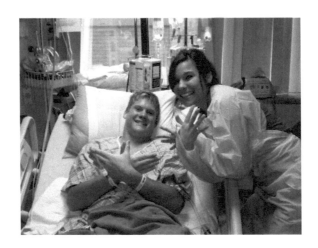

Jake, thank you for letting me share this story. God's graciousness was so evident through your calm, gentle strength. I will always be so grateful for the time we had together, learning to trust God, being patient with one another, and getting to see God work miracles. I love you, Brother. Never forget His faithfulness.

The Make A Wish foundation granted Jake a wish. He chose Hawaii because he knew how much Mom had always wanted to go. Jake also requested to bring as much as the family as possible.

My dear family, thank you for allowing the transparency among these pages. For letting me write of our vulnerabilities and fears. Thank you for encouraging me and assisting me in every way possible to make "Publishing Day" possible. I will always be grateful for shared memories.

Thank you to my husband, Rhett, for lending a listening ear, encouraging me, and being patient with me throughout this editing journey.

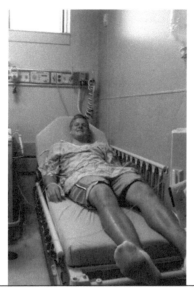

The day Jake was admitted to the hospital.
Feet hanging off the end of the bed.

Using the boflex after a chemo-treatment

I want to thank Maribelle Sharpe Hoerster (Oma) for being my beloved editor, faithful grandmother, encourager, and an amazing example of patience, love and grace.

Senior Prom 2012: Oma and Opa with Queen and King. Cousin Amanda and Jake

Mom administering the ARA-C at home.

2013 Mason's Annual Cancer Survivor Walk- Mom, Jake and Dad in front, Aunt Natalie with Oma and Aunt Lizzie in back.

[Prom 2011] His Loyal Bald Buddies: From left to right: Elliot, Dyllan, Korey, Jake, Woody, Briggs, Matt

Football Season 2010: Jake and Dad after Puncher victory. Two of the Puncher's biggest fans.

Thank you to our wonderful little community. The love and support we felt every step of the way was a huge part in keeping our hearts focused on the One True Healer.

Hawaii April 2012 "Big Belly Dance Off"

May 10th 2011- The day his hair fell out

Thank you to the Oncologists, Nurses and Staff who work endlessly, care much, and offer so much support during their patient's battle against cancer.

"Never stop fighting the good fight."

Justin and Sherryl Bibb happy parents and grandparents. Pictured right to left: <u>Davidson Family</u>: Eldest sister, Emilie and her husband Daniel with their five children, Beaux, Truett, Gillis, Wyatt and Quinn <u>Justin Bibb Junior Family</u>: Oldest Brother, (Jeb), with wife Katherine and their eldest Daughter, Sophia. (not yet born: Baby Sam Sam) <u>Tisdale Family</u>: Sister Jessica with husband Rhett (now also expecting their first child) <u>William Family</u>: Sister, Hillary with husband Todd <u>Jacob Bibb Family</u>: with new Bride, Evelyn <u>Elliot Bibb Family</u>: with wife, Cheyenne <u>The Youngest Bibb</u>: Garrett, currently working on his education in construction science